Unlocking Income with ChatGPT

Ethical AI-Driven Strategies for Wealth Generation

Table of Contents

Your Free Gift

As a way of saying thanks for your purchase, I'm offering the book **"AI For Entrepreneurs: How to Successfully Build, Grow or Expand Your Business Using Artificial Intelligence"** for FREE to my readers.

Get instant access here:
https://lp.profitablefuturewithai.com

In the free book, you will discover:

- **Unlock the Power of Artificial Intelligence Reception Etiquette:** Whether you're a fledgling startup or an established business, your operation can harness the power of AI.
- **Boost Productivity and Save Precious Time:** Success is a ticking clock. AI technology can help you cut corners without compromising on output quality. Take back

7

your office hours and see the huge positive impact on your productivity.

- **Get a Comprehensive Plan to Implement AI:** Understand exactly how to incorporate artificial intelligence into different aspects of your business. Keen insights that are quick to execute and promise to transform your business operati**ons!**

Thriving in the Business World with AI: A Must-Have Guide for Entrepreneurs

Seize the Opportunity! If you aspire to successfully build, grow or expand your business using artificial intelligence, then this free **"AI For Entrepreneurs"** book is an invaluable resource for you. It will not only help you avoid common technological pitfalls but also streamline your business growth journey. Get your **complimentary copy** today!

Introduction

The year is 2025. You wake up and are greeted by an AI assistant customized just for you. It knows your schedule, habits, and preferences better than you do. Your self-driving car seamlessly navigates morning traffic while you finish up work emails. At the office, AI algorithms monitor supply chains, manage finances, and point out inefficiencies no human could ever detect. Robots gracefully handle hazardous tasks on the factory floor as a neural network generates an ad campaign with creativity that rivals Mozart. Later, an AI doctor reviews medical scans with superhuman precision, saving lives in the process. Dinner is prepared by a robot chef and served up hot when you walk in the door. Before bed, you don your VR headset and enter a vivid, AI-generated world.

This is our future. Artificial intelligence is reinventing society right under our noses. Its rise is inevitable, its potential boundless. AI already encapsulates everything from smart assistants to self-driving cars to medical marvels. This book will chronicle the dawn of the AI revolution.

In the vast landscape of technological advancements, one phenomenon has emerged as a harbinger of transformative change. It is reshaping industries, society, and our understanding of what it means to be human. Artificial Intelligence (AI) has unprecedented capabilities to learn, reason, and adapt and has become the driving force behind a new era of innovation and human progress.

This book, "Unlocking Passive Income with ChatGPT," will take you on a journey to explore the profound impact of AI on the world, both present and future. It will delve into the remarkable achievements, limitless potential, and challenges ahead as humanity navigates this new world shaped by intelligent machines.

The transformational power of AI transcends boundaries, revolutionizing sectors as diverse as healthcare, finance, transportation, manufacturing, and entertainment. It empowers people to unlock the secrets of big data, unravel complex patterns, and make informed decisions that were once unimaginable. From personalized medicine to self-driving cars, AI is not just a buzzword but a catalyst for disruptive change, birthing a new era of efficiency, productivity, and profitability.

As an AI researcher who led teams at major tech firms for over a decade, I have witnessed firsthand the meteoric rise of artificial intelligence. When I started out, AI was seen as a niche field of research. But in recent years, transformative technologies like deep learning have unlocked its vast potential. Now, AI is pervading every industry and reshaping our lives in profound ways.

The latest AI capability that has captured the world's attention is ChatGPT, launched by research company OpenAI in November 2022. ChatGPT is a large language model trained on a massive dataset that can generate remarkably human-like text. Many believe ChatGPT represents an inflection point for AI, bringing this once distant technology into the mainstream.

This book will be your clarity amidst the AI chaos. With simple explanations and real-world context, I'll demystify AI so you can cut through the hype. You'll discover the basic principles powering today's AI innovations so you can evaluate their actual potential. Using relatable examples, I'll reveal AI's practical applications in business, healthcare, and beyond. You'll learn where AI excels, where it falls short, and the advancements that point to an intriguing future. Consider this your handy roadmap to navigating the AI revolution as an informed citizen, consumer and professional.

My decade developing AI technologies at leading companies provides insider insights beyond dusty textbooks.

To chart a prosperous future, one must also confront the ethical and societal challenges head-on. You will explore the pressing issues of AI ethics, including fairness, transparency, and accountability, while addressing the importance of diversity and inclusivity in AI development. By striking a balance between innovation and responsibility, humanity can ensure that AI works in harmony with it, augmenting its capabilities rather than replacing them.

Explore the transformative power of AI and shape a future where the limitless potential of intelligent machines harmonizes with the boundless possibilities of the human spirit!

Chapter 1: The AI Revolution

In recent years, there has been a remarkable transformation in the world of technology that revolutionized industries and reshaped the way people live and work. At the heart of this shift lies the rapid advancement and adoption of Artificial Intelligence (AI). This chapter will explore AI's profound impact and immense potential in shaping a smarter and brighter future.

The Paradigm Shift in Technology

In the past, religious doctrine heavily influenced society; knowledge was hard-won, and access to it was closely guarded. But with the dawning of the Renaissance and Enlightenment era came intellectual liberation – scholars challenged traditional beliefs through rigorous examination, sparking a monumental change in mindset.

Then came industrialization, during which science took precedence as efficiency became paramount for economic growth. Mass production boomed alongside breakthroughs from horse/buggy to airplanes, trains, and cars!

Information Technology is another major revolutionary change. It is considered one of mankind's greatest achievements, which completely changed how data is transmitted across generations via digital media platforms.

The rapid development of technology has completely transformed access to information, trading, and communication. People have gone from simply consuming facts to now being able to digest knowledge in a matter of seconds. AI is definitely one of mankind's biggest achievements over recent years. With its help, people are no longer limited to just human intelligence. Machine learning, how AI systems understand human language, and data analytics have enabled AI systems to take on complex tasks that were once impossible.

ChatGPT is at the forefront of the AI scene. This groundbreaking model will revolutionize customer service industries by allowing them to make smart decisions from automated conversations. ChatGPT is a conversational AI system trained on vast datasets and human conversations. It can generate everything from essays, emails, social media posts to research papers, business plans, and much more in seconds based on a prompt. This cuts hours or even days out of writing and creating original content.

Also, content creation can be done faster than ever before! In my opinion, this paradigm shift brought forth by ChatGPT is unprecedented in modern times. Every industry will feel its ripple effect, eventually making life easier for everyone in ways you could've never imagined possible beforehand – talk about an upgrade!

What Is Artificial Intelligence?

When you hear about Artificial Intelligence, you might think of self-driving cars, ChatGPT bots, other AI models, and realistically rendered images. But it's also important to look at the underpinnings behind all these outputs and understand how AI works as well as its implications for society.

Broadly speaking, AI can do tasks typically associated with human cognitive functions — like decoding language, playing video games, and recognizing patterns. Essentially, they learn by processing huge volumes of data in search of models that shape their decision-making process.

In many scenarios, people need to oversee an AI's training - rewarding favorable decisions while limiting bad ones - but some are designed to learn unsupervised; say, by playing a game over and over again until they get the hang of it!

The science behind programming Artificial Intelligence involves honing its cognitive skills, such as:

- **Learning**: Gathering information and constructing algorithms that provide instructions for accomplishing certain objectives

- **Reasoning**: Deciding upon the best algorithm to reach goals

- **Self-correction:** Continuously refining algorithms so accurate results can be achieved every time

- **Creativity**: Using neural networks (AI systems are structured in layers, like neurons in a brain, to filter information and make decisions) and rules-based systems, among others, to generate original content like music and text

The Four Types of AI

According to Arend Hintze, an assistant professor of integrative biology and computer science and engineering at Michigan State University, there are four major types of AI. They are:

1. **Reactive Machines**: These AI models are limited in their abilities as they have no memory and are specifically designed for certain tasks - like Deep Blue, the IBM chess program that defeated Garry Kasparov back in the 90s. It was only able to recognize pieces on a board and make predictions without any prior experience or access to stored data.

2. **Limited Memory Systems**: Unlike reactive models, which lack memory

storage, this type has short-term data retention ability, allowing it to consider past experiences when making decisions – such as those used for self-driving cars.

3. **Theory of Mind AI Systems:** This category focuses more on social intelligence by looking at emotion recognition through inference of human intentions – something necessary if robots are going to become part of daily life one day soon.

4. **Self-Awareness Models:** The ultimate goal here is achieving true machine consciousness, whereby artificial systems can identify their own current states, giving them a level of autonomy over their decision-making processes not seen before. This level hasn't been achieved yet!

AI Success Stories

AI has been the driving force behind some amazing successes. According to Harvard Business Review, Associated Press trained its AI to effortlessly write short financial news stories, which enabled them to produce 12 times more content. As a result, they freed up their journalists to focus on more in-depth pieces.

Deep Patient, a powerful tool developed by Icahn School of Medicine at Mount Sinai, can help doctors identify high-risk patients before they can even be diagnosed with an illness. This incredible technology can predict nearly 80 diseases approximately one year before their onset based on a patient's medical history.

How AI Is Transforming Industries and Revolutionizing Business Models

The business landscape is transforming dramatically. AI, machine learning, and natural language processing are now hot topics in the workplace. Businesses have their doubts about these technologies and how they could shape the future of work; this next section will give you a look into some ways that AI is changing various industries.

Agriculture

Farmers today face many challenges, from water shortages to labor crunches. ChatGPT presents an opportunity to transform farming through customized AI solutions. With the right data and prompts, ChatGPT can generate insights to boost efficiency and crop yields.

Precision agriculture uses technology to target inputs and practices. Rather than applying water, fertilizer, and pesticides uniformly across fields, precision agriculture uses AI and data to determine optimal distribution.

ChatGPT can analyze crop needs down to the square meter. With prompts on field conditions, weather, and plant health data, ChatGPT can provide custom recommendations to use resources sustainably.

For example, FarmWise leverages ChatGPT in its autonomous farming robots. By pulling data on plant health and soil moisture, FarmWise robots can weed and seed with precision.

ChatGPT can also serve as an AI agronomist. With prompts on crop varieties, climate patterns, and growth cycles, ChatGPT can generate best practices for planting, irrigation, pest management, and harvesting.

Blue River Technology uses ChatGPT-powered visual AI on its agricultural machines. By identifying plants and weeds, Blue River can target herbicide spraying precisely. This reduces chemical use over 70%.

ChatGPT is just beginning to unlock AI's potential in farming. As more ag data is collected, ChatGPT's recommendations will become more accurate and customized. Farmers should be proactive in leveraging ChatGPT now to solve problems and maximize yields sustainably.

Construction

Artificial Intelligence (AI) is revolutionizing various industries, and the construction sector is no exception. Leveraging AI solutions, like ChatGPT, can significantly reduce the time spent on planning steps by providing accurate estimates of project costs and durations.

ChatGPT's advanced machine learning algorithms can analyze historical project data to predict budgets and time frames before the commencement of work. This predictive capability can be a game-changer in the construction sector, where cost overruns and project delays are common.

To understand the practical implications of AI in construction, consider firms such as Caidio, Kwant.ai, and AirWorks. These companies are pioneering the use of AI in the construction sector:

1. **Caidio**: This company uses AI to automate concrete data analysis, enhancing the quality of construction and reducing unnecessary costs.

2. **Kwant.ai**: Kwant.ai leverages AI and predictive analytics to improve site safety and increase productivity in construction projects.

3. **AirWorks**: AirWorks uses AI-powered automation to convert aerial data into CAD (Computer-Aided Design) drafts, significantly reducing the time and effort spent on manual drafting.

ChatGPT could be utilized in the construction industry for a variety of tasks. For instance, it can be used to draft and revise project reports, analyze project data, or even interact with project management software to provide real-time updates. It can also be trained to understand the specific language and terms used in the construction industry, making it a powerful tool for automating various tasks.

Education

For teachers, AI can automate time-consuming tasks like grading assignments and tests. This frees up teachers' time, allowing them to focus more on directly engaging with students and improving lesson plans. ChatGPT and similar tools can also provide insight into common student misconceptions and struggles, helping teachers tailor their lessons accordingly.

For students, AI tutors can provide on-demand assistance, clarifying complex concepts, answering questions, and giving real-time feedback. Student learning and outcomes have been shown to improve with AI teaching aids that can adapt to individual needs and pace of learning. Carnegie Learning, Cognii, and Century Tech are all reaping the rewards of using Artificial Intelligence in education.

Finance

ChatGPT and other AI systems are playing an increasingly important role within the finance industry, helping with tasks like credit risk assessment, fraud detection, and portfolio management. When a bank evaluates a loan application, ChatGPT could analyze the numerous variables and recommend whether to approve or deny the loan based on risk factors.

For portfolio management, ChatGPT could offer insights and strategy suggestions to maximize returns while minimizing risks. It could identify investments with low correlations to provide diversification and generate possible scenarios for how the market might evolve based on historical data and current trends.

While AI cannot fully replace human judgment in finance, ChatGPT and similar conversational AI assistants are becoming valuable tools to augment the work of financial professionals. They can analyze huge amounts of data, detect patterns, and generate insights at a scale and speed that humans cannot match.

However, companies still need experts in finance and risk management to establish guidelines, evaluate the recommendations from AI systems, and make the final decisions. AI technology in finance aims to aid, rather than replace, the experts within this complex and critical industry. Companies utilizing AI across the finance industry include:

- Socure

- Scienaptic AI

- AlphaSense

Logistics

When it comes to logistics, artificial intelligence like ChatGPT can provide valuable insights and suggestions to optimize operations. ChatGPT can assist with:

1. **Supplier selection**: ChatGPT can analyze your company's supply chain and product needs to recommend suppliers that best match those requirements. It considers factors like cost, lead times, reliability, and quality to produce a ranked list of potential suppliers.

2. **Vehicle routing**: ChatGPT can generate optimized routes for delivery drivers based on package locations, destinations, and other constraints. It finds the most efficient

routes that minimize travel time, distance, and fuel costs.

3. **Package optimization**: ChatGPT can recommend optimal packing and sorting strategies based on package dimensions, weights, fragility, and other attributes. It determines the best box sizes, cushioning materials, and sorting orders to minimize wasted space and breakage.

4. **Distribution center siting**: ChatGPT can model the costs and benefits of potential distribution center locations based on factors like proximity to suppliers, customers, transportation networks, and labor markets. It helps identify sites that maximize efficiency and minimize distribution expenses.

Companies using AI in logistics include:

- Uptake

- HAVI

- Symbotic

Real Estate

Automating routines like property evaluation reports and documents creation can save agents valuable time, allowing them to focus on higher-value tasks. Agents could leverage ChatGPT to:

1. Answer buyer and seller questions quickly, building trust and rapport. ChatGPT's explanations and reasoning capabilities could alleviate clients' concerns.

2. Generate accurate and legally compliant contracts, inspection reports, and other paperwork in minutes instead of hours. This reduces workload and billing times for agents.

3. Create virtual walkthroughs and 3D models of listings using text descriptions, photos, and floor plans. ChatGPT could even suggest improvements to optimize values. Clients could experience properties virtually before committing to viewings.

4. Advise on negotiation strategies, market trends, and comparable properties based on provided details. ChatGPT's knowledge graph could integrate data from multiple listing services.

Companies using AI in the real estate industry include:

- Compass

- Zillow

- Redfin

Security

Security-wise, AI can protect confidential information and detect malicious threats like phishing or hacking attempts. Companies like Cynet, FireEye, and Blue Hexagon offer these solutions.

Exploring the Potential of AI

In November 2022, OpenAI – one of the world's leading research organizations – made history with their revolutionary tools: ChatGPT and DALL-E 2. Sundar Pichai, Google CEO, was right - Artificial Intelligence (AI) will revolutionize the future! These generators, leveraging existing data sets for input, have opened up a whole new realm of possibilities, from product design to artistry and beyond. AI has provided innovators with an incredible superpower that will surely change the game forever!

ChatGPT is based on GenAI technology which can turn user inputs into audio files, code snippets, or even videos with remarkable accuracy. And then there's DALL-E 2 - converting images into 3D objects with unprecedented precision - allowing people to explore further than ever before! It's no surprise tech giants are vying for pole position as they race ahead in this new era; Microsoft made a huge statement recently, splashing 10 billion dollars on OpenAI to incorporate ChatGPT within their Edge browser and Bing search engine. This move is set to shake up Google's longtime web monopoly.

The impact AI has had since its inception is truly remarkable; from marketing strategies through software development all the way down to architecture - no sphere remains unaffected. Although some may see it as an intimidating or threatening force, it brings opportunity, too - enabling progress like never before and ushering in a new wave of creativity and possibility.

One of the most common questions when it comes to Artificial Intelligence is whether it can ever supersede the capabilities of humans - this suggests that people are equals in the grand scheme of things. However, this is not accurate. Machines powered by AI have a major benefit over people; speed, accuracy, and reliability.

On the other hand, though, people have invaluable qualities such as emotionality and intuition, which allows people to comprehend cultural intricacies better than any machine could ever hope to. Human instinctual abilities have been crucial for societal growth, while those who solely depend on technology get left behind in comparison. To ensure future success, it's imperative to incorporate advancements from tech and humanity's organic gifts into one cohesive plan for progress.

The Role of AI in Maximizing Earnings and Creating Passive Income

Generating passive income has never been simpler - and with the help of AI, you can set up passive income streams. Investing in stocks is a classic way to make money without having to grind at a 9 to 5 job, but harnessing machine learning algorithms takes it up another notch. These tools are designed for data analysis and predicting which investments will yield substantial returns so you have an edge when making choices. Plus, utilizing AI saves time from traditional methods of researching stocks while keeping your portfolio diversified for maximum success.

Chatbots also provide immense opportunities for earning passive income. Businesses can set up automated customer service systems that save time by not requiring someone to actively engage with customers. Plus, if coding or software development is your jam, why not sell chatbot products or services?

Also, don't forget about advertising platforms powered by AI - they're great for optimizing campaigns and ensuring that ads efficiently reach those who need them.

Finally, affiliate marketing presents another excellent chance to use AI technology to maximize earnings from each campaign. By leveraging advanced tools driven by Artificial Intelligence, it's easy enough for novices.

Embracing AI: A Mindset for Success

In this tech-driven era, growth is non-negotiable. With groundbreaking developments happening on a daily basis and cutting-edge solutions becoming increasingly sophisticated, staying ahead of the competition can be daunting. Succeeding in today's landscape requires you to have an open mindset. Any obstacle you face should be viewed as a learning experience. AI doesn't have to cause fear but rather a tool you can take advantage of. Embracing change will offer countless opportunities, so take advantage while you still can.

An Example of Harnessing AI for Career Advancement

My friend Zaroon started using ChatGPT at his tech company and it transformed how he worked. Initially, he was like any other Account Executive - working hard to hit targets and keep up with his workload. But after discovering ChatGPT, Zaroon became fascinated with artificial intelligence.

Seeing how I leveraged AI tools to boost performance, Zaroon couldn't resist exploring it himself. He researched lead generation tactics, content creation hacks, and customer research strategies to get a competitive edge.

ChatGPT allowed Zaroon to analyze consumer trends more effectively and create tailored sales pitches that impressed everyone. With ChatGPT automating tedious tasks faster than ever, he freed up more time for strategic planning. The result? A huge spike in productivity beyond all expectations.

Experts estimate 47% of jobs in the next decade will need reimagining as AI like ChatGPT becomes more prevalent. But it doesn't have to replace people! With an AI mindset that sees it as an opportunity rather than a threat, humans can enhance their skills and performance.

Take Zaroon - he recognized ChatGPT's potential early on. This enabled him to build a powerful sales engine augmented by AI, proving the power of a growth mindset.

The key to an AI mindset is accepting that it:

- Automates routine tasks so you can focus on high-value work

- Combines human expertise with machine capabilities

- Develops thoughtful solutions through creative problem solving

Adopting this mindset is essential as companies keep pace in our fast-changing world.

Chapter 2: Demystifying Artificial Intelligence

The previous chapter gave you an idea of how AI is transforming the world. This chapter will focus on the concept of machine learning, a driving force behind AI's astonishing capabilities. Understanding the algorithms that enable machines to learn from data and improve their performance over time is crucial in comprehending the underlying mechanisms of AI.

Unleashing the Power of Artificial Intelligence

Machine learning algorithms enable computers to discover valuable patterns in data and make accurate predictions without being explicitly programmed. ChatGPT relies on machine learning models throughout its system to provide relevant and helpful responses.

Supervised learning methods allow ChatGPT to comprehend written questions accurately by training on large datasets of labeled text. These models learn from examples of correct input-output pairs to determine how to respond to new inputs. ChatGPT likely uses neural networks and natural language processing techniques for supervised learning tasks like question answering.

ChatGPT's responses also emerge from its ability to detect patterns in unlabeled datasets using unsupervised learning algorithms. Clustering and dimensionality reduction models allow ChatGPT to organize knowledge, analyze user conversations, and identify common themes. This helps inform ChatGPT's navigation of complex topics.

ChatGPT's continuing improvements likely stem from reinforcement learning. When users provide positive feedback on ChatGPT's responses, it informs the reinforcement learning algorithms to reward that behavior and generate similarly helpful answers in the future. This iterative process allows ChatGPT to learn from interactions over time.

Ensemble learning methods appear essential for balancing ChatGPT's nuanced and complex responses. By combining the predictions from many machine learning models, ChatGPT's overall accuracy and robustness improve. This aggregation of results further enables ChatGPT to discuss complex, multifaceted topics in reasonable and thoughtful ways.

The Fuel That Drives AI Innovation

As businesses are pushed to keep up with the ever-changing digital landscape, data has become more essential than ever when it comes to driving innovation and staying competitive. Without access to timely and relevant information, companies risk getting left behind in the dust.

That's why utilizing Artificial Intelligence (AI) is so important - harnessing its power can unlock a wealth of insights from large datasets that would otherwise be difficult or impossible for humans alone to process quickly enough.

By leveraging AI systems, organizations have an opportunity like never before to gain a deeper understanding of customer behavior and preferences while revolutionizing how they deliver experiences no one even knew existed.

Microsoft sums it up best: "The promise of AI is that knowledge gained from applying analytics will enhance any decision-making process with additional intelligence, helping us produce quicker, more effective outcomes." It's true – if you want your business on top of the game now and in years to come, don't ignore this invaluable asset.

The Data Dilemma

Almost every customer I come across has a high interest in addressing two questions:

1. How should we effectively utilize data to make more intelligent and well-informed decisions?

2. What steps should we take to enhance the capabilities of AI and data science?

Recent findings provide evidence of the immense importance of gathering and analyzing information for businesses today. To underscore this sentiment, here are some statistics worth considering:

- A 10 percent increase in accessible data can potentially result in an additional $65 million worth of net income for the average Fortune 1000 company.

- According to New Vantage Partners' Big Data Executive Survey, 85% of companies desire their operations to be driven by insights derived from analysis- although only about 37 percent have achieved this successfully.

- AI systems hold tremendous potential in making sense of the vast amounts of available but untapped information - highlighting the need to embrace this trend right away.

The Fuel That Runs Business

Data is no longer the waste product of a business process; it's become the essential fuel that drives forward momentum. According to Accenture, AI has been estimated to double economic growth and increase labor productivity by up to 40% by 2035. Utilizing this technology could be key for any leader looking to succeed in a rapidly changing world.

Augmented intelligence provides the tools to enhance human capabilities, while innovations like AI allow algorithms like facial recognition to work without needing an internet connection. The Artificial Intelligence Index Report states that computing power grows exponentially every 3.4 months. Its effectiveness has been seen during Covid-19 with quicker diagnosis, vaccine development, and treatment protocols being implemented faster than ever before, thanks in part due to these advancements in technology.

That said, the ethical implications of introducing large-scale Artificial Intelligence need to be taken into consideration. Whether it be from brands or personal use - there needs to be some form of governance over these technologies if they're going to be used responsibly and not have potentially negative impacts on humanity as a whole. It's becoming increasingly important for leaders everywhere to understand how best to work alongside intelligent machines rather than against them to ensure future success both personally and professionally.

It's time to break down the importance of data collection:

Data Is a Game Changer

Having access to good data means having all the power you need to make informed decisions and take full advantage of any opportunity that comes your way. Not only will reliable data give you a strong case when it comes to backing up those choices, but it will also prevent mistakes or jumping to wrong conclusions.

Uncover Problems with Data

No matter the organization, there are bound to be issues lurking around somewhere - so why not do your best to uncover them? With accurate figures and facts, one can quickly identify potential problems – saving everyone from future headaches, all while staying one step ahead.

The Accuracy of a Good Model

Solid information leads to developing more precise theories for longer-term solutions that can actually work in real-life situations - because, let's face it, without knowing what happens within our operations, it would be hard (if not impossible) to make anything happen successfully with just guesswork involved. Data gives an edge by providing those building blocks necessary for constructing coherent models showing everything as clear as day.

Back Up Your Arguments with Facts and Figures

Everyone has their opinion these days. However, making positive changes within a company isn't easy if most people don't agree with you immediately. However, if you arm yourself well enough by presenting sound evidence alongside reasoning, chances are much higher for getting approval. After all, nothing makes a statement stronger than factual numbers do.

Data Makes Your Strategy Strategic

Are you ever uncertain of where to focus your efforts? Gaining insight through data collection is the key to success and eliminating any doubts. The most prosperous organizations have short-term and long-term objectives in place. With comprehensive data gathering and analysis, you can trust that your resources are being used in the best way possible. Knowing which areas require extra attention will take an organization from good to great. So don't be left behind; get a handle on exactly what needs improvement with detailed data collection.

Funding Is Much Easier When You Have Data

These days it pays off (literally) when organizations can demonstrate their outcomes with evidence-based practices; this means reliable data collection systems are a must for any moneymaker out there. No more relying on hunches or assumptions -

having concrete facts at hand gives everyone involved the confidence that comes with knowing what needs doing and how best to approach it.

Knowing What Works Well Puts You Ahead of the Curve

Collecting data isn't all about identifying weaknesses; knowing one's strengths is just as important. By analyzing what works well, leaders can replicate these successes across different parts of their operations for maximum impact. Seeing who's excelling lets decision-makers pinpoint high performers so they learn how other departments could benefit from similar methods.

Saving Time

A comprehensive system designed around fast access makes life much easier down the line. Having everything organized ahead of time saves valuable energy by cutting out repetitive tasks such as manually inputting information each time somebody asks for it.

Preparing Data for AI

While ChatGPT and other AI systems show great promise, they ultimately depend on the quality of the data and training they receive.

ChatGPT's responses are only as good as the data that went into creating and refining its neural networks and machine learning models. If

ChatGPT's training data contains biases, inconsistencies, or other issues, those will likely carry through to its responses.

Businesses looking to utilize ChatGPT or build their own AI systems must focus first on collecting and curating high-quality data and training sets. Without well-organized, accurate and representative data, even the most advanced AI algorithms will struggle to produce useful output.

The inputs fed into ChatGPT shape its knowledge base and ability to understand language and provide helpful responses. Garbage in leads to garbage out. To truly unlock the potential of AI like ChatGPT, companies must invest in data governance, cleaning and labeling processes to prepare well-organized datasets.

As ChatGPT continues to learn and improve, regular auditing and refinement of its training data will be necessary to mitigate biases, correct misconceptions and improve relevance. An emphasis on the data lifecycle - from collection to training to refinement - will be key for getting the most value from AI systems like ChatGPT.

Over the past few months, I have gained valuable insights from ChatGPT and its capabilities. From observing ChatGPT's responses and limitations, I believe there will need to be a focus on "data for the AI lifecycle" to truly advance large-scale AI models like ChatGPT.

ChatGPT only has access to the data that OpenAI's scientists have fed into its training data. However, to achieve broader and more accurate responses, ChatGPT will need access to a wider range of high-quality data at all stages of its "life." This includes data for:

• Initial model training

• Continual learning and updates

• Testing and evaluation

• Debugging and error analysis

To provide ChatGPT with this full "AI lifecycle data," OpenAI and other AI companies will need to establish partnerships with data providers, annotation services, and other AI players who specialize in different types of data. They will also need to build seamless interfaces that allow new data to be easily ingested by the models.

If OpenAI can successfully acquire and integrate relevant data at each stage of ChatGPT's development, they may be able to significantly reduce the 80% of scientists' time currently spent sorting, labeling and annotating data. This "AI lifecycle data" approach has the potential to dramatically accelerate ChatGPT's progress by feeding it a more robust, continuously updating knowledge base.

You need to understand each step in its data lifecycle to get the most out of your investment in Artificial Intelligence (AI). Here are four essential processes that will ensure success when working with AI data.

1. **Data Sourcing**: Finding reliable sources for your data is key, whether it be custom datasets from trusted vendors or pre-labeled collections. Quality control is also paramount, as poor-quality information can lead to erroneous results down the line.

2. **Data Preparation**: To maximize accuracy and minimize bias during model training and deployment, preparation stages such as annotation and quality assurance must take place before advancing further into the cycle. A strong knowledge graph and ontology also help boost overall performance too!

3. **Model Training and Deployment**: As hard work has been done on stage two, this process should run relatively smoothly – but don't forget about human evaluation post-implementation. It's important to continually evaluate models so they remain accurate over time and free from prejudice

opinions or decisions being made by machines alone.

4. **Evaluation by Humans**: Keep tabs on how well your algorithms are doing at predicting outcomes through careful manual inspection. Make sure there's no hidden bias based on learned patterns that could mess up future inferences.

Having an understanding of each phase involved in an AI's data lifecycle will guarantee successful use cases both now and in the future.

Data Preparation: A Key Element to AI Success

Getting the data ready is essential for any successful Artificial Intelligence project. Labeling each dataset correctly and running it through a quality assurance process to guarantee labeling accuracy must be done with precision. Data preparation can be done in-house or via an external partner, either by hand or using smart annotation technology, which merges human and machine annotation techniques.

Model Training and Deployment

Integrating your data source with your model infrastructure will ensure a smooth transition from the earlier stages all the way up until the deployment stage, making development easier as well as ongoing training programs simpler.

Evaluation by Humans

The last step involves continuous testing, retraining, and assessing the model to guarantee its performance under real-world scenarios. Benchmarking against other models available on the market also helps keep track of changing trends over time. Improvements can then be made when necessary, without becoming obsolete due to 'data drift' resulting from environmental evolution or user changes affecting both the model itself and its users.

How to Take Your Data to the Next Level

You already know the value data holds for AI, but how can you maximize it? Here are a few pointers to ensure your company's data is always at peak performance:

- **Streamline the annotation process with ML-assisted labeling**: Integrating machine learning and human annotators provides an efficient and cost-effective way of preparing data - plus, it can even guarantee greater accuracy.

- **Leverage secure cloud storage when sharing info**: Moving large amounts of data takes time; make life easier by using cloud storage to securely transfer information.

Hardware and Software Infrastructure for AI Development

As IT prepares for an AI future with models like ChatGPT, they must decide how to set up hardware for AI systems. Hyper-converged systems are attractive because they are compact, flexible, and can grow easily. ChatGPT and other AI models need lots of computing power, but the hardware setup is similar to traditional hyper-converged systems. IT just needs more computing power and faster networks to handle the demands of large AI models.

AI Requirements and Core Components

You need to clean your data by filtering, categorizing and selecting important features. You often need to combine multiple datasets into one big dataset.

You need fast and large storage to save your prepared data. But the storage needs are not the same as the computing needs. ChatGPT and other AI models need much more computing power than storage space. So you should design your AI system to separate the storage from the computing hardware. This allows you to scale them independently based on your specific needs.

System Requirements and Components

For AI to reach its peak performance, there are a few key components you'll need:

1. **CPUs**: When it comes to VM or container subsystems, dispatching code to GPUs, and managing I/O, the best options on the market right now are either 2nd-gen Xeon Scalable Platinum or Gold processors from Intel - but if you're looking for something more cost-effective that still packs a punch AMD Epyc CPUs (2nd Gen Rome) have been making serious waves recently. Plus, with their added features designed specifically for ML and DL inference operations, these chips are essential for production AI workloads powered by previously trained models on GPUs.

2. **GPUs**: Nvidia P100 (Pascal), V100 (Volta), and A100 (Ampere) will get your training done, while V100, A100, and T4(Turing) can handle inferencing easily - though AMD has yet to make significant gains with Instinct Vega GPU. But fear not! Several OEM products exist in both 1U-4U form factors as well as OCP 21-inch versions too, so there should be no problem finding an option that works best for you.

3. **Memory Capacity**: ML/DL processing runs off of GPU memory, meaning DRAM isn't typically much of a bottleneck; nowadays, anything between 128GB - 512GB is standard, depending on the type of system specs you decide on. The latest generation of advanced GPUs incorporates HBM modules which range from 16GB up to 32 GB – plus even 40 GB when it comes down to higher-end models like A10x – creating huge amounts of aggregate memory space considering 8 GPU systems can hold up to 256GB or 320BG worth respectively.

4. **Network Connectivity**: Nowadays, since many AI tasks require multiple server clusters working together, having fast 10gig+ Ethernet connections is imperative. That allows for quick data transfers between storage and compute subsystems that don't become bottlenecks slowing down progress significantly, giving all other operational loads time enough to breathe appropriately along the way. InfiniBand and NVLink dedicated interfaces are also available depending upon the chosen system requirements respectively here too.

5. **Storage IO Performance**: To ensure continued high speeds across long-term projects where large datasets need quick

processing times, local NVMe drives are used instead of SATA SSDs.

AI Development Frameworks and Tools

Artificial Intelligence has revolutionized the way data is collected and utilized. With its growth, a plethora of ML and AI frameworks have been released for developers to take advantage of. These technologies are:

1. Scikit-learn

This open-source library written in Python was launched in 2007 with the goal of making Machine Learning more accessible even if one doesn't possess expertise in coding languages such as Java or C++. It provides efficient ways to tackle both supervised and unsupervised learning problems under a BSD license with minimal dependencies.

Its user-friendly interface allows users unfamiliar with advanced programming languages to capitalize on it quickly, making it all the rage among professionals and students alike; plus, its API calls can be used by any algorithm within Scikit Learn, making this tool highly useful.

2. Tensorflow

Tensorflow's versatility shines through with its compatibility with both CPUs and GPUs, meaning there's no need for complex coding in C++ or CUDA to maintain GPU performance. Its interconnected network of nodes lets users quickly construct powerful artificial neural networks that can handle massive datasets - famously used by Google for their image-recognition and speech-processing applications.

3. Theano

Theano, a popular open-source Python library dedicated to deep learning, makes designing complicated neural networks a breeze. By abstracting away layers and hidden layers, you're able to train AI models on your GPU without having to sweat the small stuff. Facebook has already seen great success using Theano as they look into training and deploying their own Artificial Intelligence programs.

4. Caffe

Berkeley AI Research brings this incredible deep learning framework that is all about expression, speediness, and modularity - helping you design configuration-based models optimally without manually writing any code at all. It offers easy switching between CPU or GPU processing power so it doesn't matter if you're testing out cutting-edge NNs or creating intelligent apps; Caffe really is changing the game when it comes to research into Artificial Intelligence.

5. CNTK

The CNTK open-source framework is a quick, more versatile neural network for text, message, and voice reformatting. It offers a speedy overall assessment of the machine models while still ensuring accuracy - making it an ideal tool for scaling up operations.

With its user-friendly design and integration with massive datasets, this technology has become the go-to choice for big names like Skype, Cortana, etc.

6. OpenNN

OpenNN gives users the power of advanced analytics, enabling them to go from complete novice to pro in no time. Neural Designer is included and provides visuals like graphs and tables for a more comprehensive understanding of your data.

Plus, with its cutting-edge technology, you can dive into any analysis you want. In short: OpenNN allows anyone – regardless of experience level – access to sophisticated analytics that they can rely on at all times!

Exploring AI Algorithms and Models

In 2022, the Artificial Intelligence industry was flourishing - worth an incredible $120 billion. AI is a multifaceted branch of computer science that allows machines to think and act as humans do.

Data scientists and software engineers can now access some very advanced models.

1. ANN (Artificial Neural Network)

Think of ANNs as small computer brains; they take in information and then process it through many layers composed of nodes connected with synapses - which serve as pathways for transmitting data from one node to another for further processing. In other words, ANNs replicate how neurons operate.

2. CNN (Convolutional Neural Network)

CNN is primarily used for image recognition projects due to its ability to identify objects or features within input images via convolution layers instead of just depending on matrix multiplication alone. It can be applied in tasks such as facial identification systems, natural language understanding programs, and more.

3. RNN (Recurrent Neural Network)

RNNs remember past inputs by using their internal memory when performing future calculations or decisions – this makes them perfect tools for analyzing patterns over time such as speech recognition applications or handwriting analysis programs.

4. GAN (Generative Adversarial Networks)

GANs mimic existing patterns by synthesizing input data with analogous output results – essentially creating outputs based on what was previously observed. This model specializes in generating 'fake' content, such as images created from scratch, thanks to its two networks: The Generator and Discriminator, working together harmoniously under the hood.

5. SVM (Support Vector Machines)

Support Vector Machines simplify the ability to analyze data points even if they are spread across multiple dimensions simultaneously, thanks to its set of hyper planes mapping out boundaries between separate classes/categories within a dataset. SVMs have been used successfully in highly demanding areas like facial pose estimation and fraud detection due COVID-19 pandemic, proving just how powerful this tool can be in solving challenging issues needing accuracy, precision, and speed simultaneously!

As AI continues to become more and more prevalent, developers and users alike need to stay up-to-date on the latest AI models out there. From self-driving cars navigating city streets with ease to facial recognition software that's a part of everyday life - each model has been crafted to solve specific problems in unique ways. Whether you're trying to detect objects or estimate poses, a solid understanding of these state-of-the-art solutions will ensure success in today's technology landscape. In other words: if you want results? Know your model!

The Role of Cloud Computing in AI Development

Cloud computing is a must for businesses aiming to stay ahead of the curve. This technology provides an unprecedented level of agility, flexibility, and cost savings by storing data and applications in the cloud. But the AI capabilities are truly allowing companies to unlock their full potential – becoming more efficient, strategic, and insightful than ever before.

Cloud Delivery Models

Cloud delivery models are revolutionizing how businesses operate, allowing AI experts to get a fully functional computing environment instantly. Thanks to IaaS (Infrastructure as a Service), these specialists can instantly access CPU, memory, disc, network, and operating systems without breaking a sweat.

Plus, with PaaS (Platform as a Service), they're able to quickly create applications through data science services such as Jupyter notebooks and data catalogs – talk about saving time!

For SaaS users, life is a breeze - they get to take advantage of AI services within their favorite apps like CRM or payment processing software in no time. It's almost like having your own personal assistant but with even greater savings since data and apps are hosted on the cloud. You could say that utilizing cloud capabilities is akin to plugging into The Matrix when it comes to streamlining operations with insights-driven strategies.

The Power of Kubernetes

Data science projects heavily rely on data, which makes access an important factor for evaluating algorithms and models. That's where Kubernetes comes in handy; it deploys containerized applications across multiple cloud providers without needing any computer infrastructure setup or management help!

Plus, containers make collaborations easier by providing everyone involved with one unified interface. For secure storage of both public and private information on the cloud, you need to be aware of modern tech trends such as those involving Kubernetes - so don't let limited staff knowledge impede your digital transformation journey.

Highly Skilled Professionals Wanted

Data science and Artificial Intelligence engineering have become top contenders for higher education lately – ranging from undergraduate programs to graduate studies – with courses ranging from mathematics to computer sciences available globally. In addition, competitive marketplaces such as Kaggle and CrowdANALYTIX offer experts specialties, including deep learning specialists or natural language masters, a platform wherein they can easily work together while competing against each other. If you're looking at making strides toward success, look no further than these two fields: Data Science and Artificial Intelligence Engineering.

The rise of these platforms also brings about an exciting opportunity: a chance for smart minds around the world to grow together through shared information - creating new possibilities within data analysis for those who take advantage of it.

DevOps

DevOps has revolutionized IT operations and software development, bringing forth many advantages to creating a microservices architecture. This practice is no longer novel but rather an established approach that can't be overlooked. Although DevOps isn't designed to tackle challenges faced during Data Science life cycles, in 2018, Gartner brought us one step closer by introducing ModelOps - or Machine Learning

Operations (MLOps) for short - as an extension of DevOps.

Today's major cloud providers like Amazon Web Services (AWS), Microsoft Azure, Google Cloud Platform (GCP), IBM Cloud, and Oracle Cloud Infrastructure (OCI) have all jumped on board the AI train, offering comprehensive sets of APIs and platforms built specifically for data science and machine learning applications such as natural language processing, computer vision and automated ML solutions with both cloud-based implementations and Kubernetes infrastructures available on premises too. Companies like IBM SAS RapidMiner are also leading the charge when it comes to developing new services catered toward this growing trend.

Here are some of the key benefits of AI's widespread usage:

A Sense of Autonomy

Cloud computing combined with the power of Artificial Intelligence can help businesses become more data-driven and strategic. By automating time-consuming, repetitive tasks and data processing that don't need human participation, people can work more efficiently, enabling higher productivity overall. IT teams could use AI to supervise and oversee key activities, allowing humans to focus on the value-adding elements they specialize in.

You Don't Have to Break the Bank for Efficiency

Scaling up your operations doesn't have to mean scaling up expenses, either. Cloud computing is far more economical than having an entire onsite server room, thanks to its lack of hardware maintenance costs. Although launching an AI effort may be expensive initially, you could always opt for monthly payments as opposed to one lump sum payment (perfect if you want a cost-effective way without compromising quality or capability). What's even better? With no human assistance required, these systems are capable enough when it comes to crunching numbers and give out conclusions without any extra expenditure from your end.

Data Management Made Easy

The most crucial sectors like organization management administration or data processing have been revolutionized by Artificial Intelligence (AI). Drawing insights from real-time updates makes operations much smoother while cutting down time wasted during analysis; needless to discuss what this means for performance improvements at large-scale organizations.

Finally, gathering, organizing, and updating information has never been easier due to advanced tech like AI, which streamlines the whole process in almost no time whatsoever. It ensures all those tedious chores get done quickly and accurately so everyone involved can move ahead faster.

Chapter 3: Making Smart Financial Decisions

In this chapter, you will learn about the transformative power of Artificial Intelligence in the realm of personal finance. As technology continues to evolve, it presents a wealth of opportunities for individuals seeking to optimize their financial decision-making.

AI-Driven Budgeting and Financial Planning

ChatGPT and other AI tools are revolutionizing the financial planning industry. The ability of these models to analyze data, identify patterns and generate personalized insights at scale means financial advisors can obtain information and generate strategies in minutes that previously took days or weeks.

For financial advisors, ChatGPT provides ultra-fast data analysis and research capabilities. The model's ability to review information and documents in seconds means that tasks like researching investments, reviewing contracts and analyzing data sets are expedited dramatically compared to traditional human research methods.

ChatGPT's advantages go beyond speed. Its insights are based on analyzing enormous data sets that no human could comprehend in full. This allows the model to identify subtle patterns and correlations that a financial planner might miss. The model can then use these insights to create customized financial strategies optimized for an individual client's goals, risk tolerance and financial situation.

While ChatGPT cannot replace human advisors entirely, it has the potential to dramatically augment their capabilities. Advisors can spend less time on mundane research tasks and more time focusing on counseling clients by utilizing insights from ChatGPT. The model's impartiality and vast knowledge graph also make it well-suited to identify options a human might overlook.

Here are some tips you can use to build an AI-powered expense tracking and budgeting chatbot with ChatGPT:

1. Start by structuring the conversational flow of the chatbot. Think about the key features it should have like adding expenses, setting budgets, viewing reports etc. Map out the dialogue flow.

2. Use ChatGPT itself to generate code snippets for building the chatbot. Ask it to provide example code for things like capturing user input, storing data,

generating reports etc. in your preferred coding language.

3. Build the basic chatbot framework first - this handles the conversational flow and integrates ChatGPT responses. Popular frameworks include Dialogflow, Lex, Python libraries like ChatterBot.

4. Integrate ChatGPT API to allow generating personalized responses. You will need a valid API key. Build intents and entities so ChatGPT can understand user questions.

5. Create a database to store user expense data. You can use Google Sheets, MySQL, MongoDB etc. Write logic to save user inputs.

6. Display reports and graphs summarizing expenses, budgets etc. You can use Python visualization libraries like Matplotlib or JavaScript charting libraries.

7. Add authentication so only paid subscribers can access the full functionality. Use solutions like Auth0, Firebase Auth.

8. Host the chatbot online so it is publicly accessible. Platforms like AWS, GCP, Azure have services to deploy chatbots.

9. Start testing with sample conversations. Fix any errors and improve conversational flow. Get friends to try it out and give feedback.

10. Set up a payment gateway like Stripe to manage subscriptions. Provide pricing plans for different features.

Focus on building an MVP first before adding more advanced features. Leverage pre-built libraries and ChatGPT itself to speed up development.

AI-Powered Investment Strategies and Wealth Management

The investment management sector is currently undergoing a significant transformation, spearheaded by AI and machine learning technologies. As financial markets continue to increase in complexity, traditional investing strategies often fall short. In this new landscape, AI has emerged as a crucial tool for portfolio optimization, enabling fund managers to make data-driven decisions that yield higher returns.

One of the most promising applications of AI in this field is leveraging the capabilities of ChatGPT for predictive modeling. ChatGPT can process and interpret vast amounts of data from diverse sources, such as market data, financial statements, news articles, and social media posts. The outcome is the generation of accurate forecasts about stock prices and market trends.

With the assistance of ChatGPT, fund managers are not just reacting to market changes, but predicting and planning for them. This paradigm shift from reactive to proactive investing is a key advantage of using AI for portfolio optimization. It allows investment professionals to stay ahead of the curve, making informed decisions based on a comprehensive analysis of current market conditions, historical data, and projected trends.

Moreover, the utilization of ChatGPT is not just limited to market predictions. It can also be used as a tool for passive income, enabling individuals to establish a consistent revenue stream by leveraging the AI's predictive capabilities. For instance, small-scale investors can use ChatGPT to guide their investment strategies, helping them identify profitable opportunities and avoid potential risks. Similarly, AI-driven investment platforms can use ChatGPT to provide personalized investment advice to their users, generating income through subscription fees or commission on trades.

In conclusion, the integration of AI and machine learning technologies, specifically ChatGPT, into the investment management sector is not just transforming how fund managers optimize their portfolios, but also creating opportunities for passive income. As these technologies continue to evolve and improve, their potential applications in finance and investment will only increase, offering unprecedented opportunities for both active investors and those seeking passive income.

Here one idea you can use is to build AI-powered stock/crypto trading bots. You can use ChatGPT to generate python code for algorithmic trading bots that automate buying and selling based on technical indicators. The bots can run 24/7 and earnings can be a source of passive income.

Below am breaking down the process into simple steps to give you an idea. I assume that you have a basic understanding of Python and how to use APIs.

Step 1: Setting Up Your Environment

Firstly, you need to set up a Python environment. You can do this using Anaconda, a popular Python distribution for data science. You'll also need to install a few libraries, including requests for making HTTP requests, pandas for handling data, matplotlib for plotting data, and yfinance for fetching stock data. You can install these with the following command:

```
pip install requests pandas
matplotlib yfinance openai
```

Step 2: Getting Your API Keys

You'll need API keys for both the stock/crypto exchange you'll be trading on, and for OpenAI's GPT-3.

For the trading exchange, the process for getting an API key will depend on the exchange. Generally, you'll need to sign up, enable API access in the settings, and then generate a new API key.

For OpenAI's GPT-3, you can sign up on the OpenAI website and navigate to the API section to get your key.

Step 3: Fetching Stock/Crypto Data

Next, you'll need to fetch the stock or crypto data that you'll be trading. You can do this using the yfinance library if you're trading stocks. For cryptos, you'll need to use the API provided by your exchange. Here's an example of how you might fetch stock data:

```
import yfinance as yf

data     =     yf.download('AAPL',
start='2023-01-01',    end='2023-
12-31')
```

Step 4: Generating Trading Signals with GPT-3

Next, you can use GPT-3 to generate trading signals. These signals tell your bot when to buy or sell. You might instruct GPT-3 to generate signals based on technical indicators like the moving average or relative strength index (RSI). Here's an example:

```
import openai

openai.api_key = 'your-api-key'

response                    =
openai.Completion.create(

    engine="text-davinci-002",

    prompt="Given    the    following
stock  data,  when  should  I  buy  or
sell?\n\n" + data.to_string(),

    max_tokens=100)

print(response.choices[0].text.s
trip())
```

Step 5: Executing Trades

Once you have your trading signal, you can execute trades using the API provided by your exchange.

The specifics will depend on your exchange, but here's an example of how you might do it:

```
import requests

def           execute_trade(symbol,
action, quantity):

    url    =    'https://api.your-
exchange.com/v1/orders'

    headers   =   {'Content-Type':
'application/json',   'X-API-KEY':
'your-api-key'}

    data   =   {'symbol':   symbol,
'side':   action,   'quantity':
quantity, 'type': 'market'}

    response   =   requests.post(url,
headers=headers, json=data)

    response.raise_for_status()

execute_trade('AAPL', 'buy', 1)
```

Step 6: Monitoring and Adjusting Your Bot

Finally, you'll need to monitor your bot and adjust it as necessary. You might want to tweak your GPT-3 prompts to generate different types of signals, or adjust the parameters of your trading strategy. Be sure to keep an eye on your bot's performance and make changes as necessary.

This is a basic overview of how you might build an AI-powered trading bot. There are many other considerations, such as error handling, logging, and more. You'll also want to thoroughly test your bot in a simulated environment before letting it trade with real money. Remember, trading involves risk, and you should only trade with money you can afford to lose.

ChatGPT for Trading and Stock Market Predictions

The investment management industry is going through a major shift, and it's all thanks to ChatGPT. As financial markets become more intricate, traditional methods are becoming obsolete - making Artificial Intelligence an absolute must for portfolio optimization.

Utilizing Artificial Intelligence has enabled fund managers to build sophisticated predictive models that are capable of crunching through immense amounts of data from various sources: market info, financial statements, news stories, or social media posts - all of which generate accurate predictions about asset prices and trends in order to make informed decisions when managing investments or constructing portfolios.

Investors now have access to greater insight into what's happening on the stock exchange. With these new tools at their disposal, money-managers can better optimize their strategies and get high returns on investments.

Creating a passive income stream using ChatGPT for trading and stock market predictions involves several steps. However, it's important to keep in mind that no AI or machine learning model can guarantee profit in the stock market. The stock market is influenced by a wide range of factors, many of which are unpredictable and not included in historical data. Furthermore, using AI for financial trading involves a high risk and should only be done with money you can afford to lose.

Below are the steps you can take to set up such a system:

1. Train a model on financial data. This would involve processing historical stock market data and financial news data, and then using this data to train the model. It's important to include as many relevant factors as possible, such as company earnings, economic indicators, and geopolitical events.

2. Create an API for your model. This API would take in relevant data (for example,

today's financial news and the current stock prices) and output the model's predictions.

3. Integrate the API with ChatGPT. You would likely want to create a custom implementation of ChatGPT that can understand questions about stock market predictions and respond with the predictions from your model.

4. There are several ways to monetize your ChatGPT application:

- **Subscription Service**: Users pay a monthly fee to access your chatbot.

- **Pay-Per-Use**: Users pay each time they use your chatbot.

- **Advertising**: Display relevant advertisements on your chatbot's interface.

Remember that it's important to clearly communicate to users that your chatbot's predictions are not guaranteed to be accurate and that investing in the stock market always involves risk.

Other than this you can use ChatGPT to analyze a client's financial situation and goals to generate a personalized financial plan covering budgeting, taxes, investments etc. This of course will be a paid service.

Fraud Detection and Identity Protection

It's no secret that identity theft is a growing issue in the US. According to Javelin's 2018 Identity Fraud study, a record 16.7 million American adults were affected last year—a whopping 8% increase from the previous 12 months. With hackers and fraudsters getting more sophisticated, the number of fraudulent transactions is only going up.

Fortunately, there are ID scanning solutions to combat this problem; some simply scan an ID's barcode, while other advanced methods perform forensic and biometric tests for extra security measures. But these can be made even better with machine learning tools and Artificial Intelligence.

Here are five popular use cases of ML for fraud detection:

1. Online Stores and Transaction Fraud

With shoppers racking up billions of dollars in losses due to online fraud, retail websites must stay vigilant when processing orders and related payments — especially since AI tech makes it easier to detect anomalies or any suspicious activity quickly.

2. Financial Institutions, Fintechs, and Insurers

For financial institutions, fintech companies, and insurance providers alike, there's one thing that remains true: meeting compliance regulations is key. In other words - they need to ensure that their customers are legitimate, not fraudulent actors.

But speed can be a challenge in making this happen; it can be hard to keep up with the competition while also double-checking account holders. That's where machine learning systems come into play! By analyzing data points associated with suspicious behavior quickly and accurately – these organizations get an invaluable window into what makes a real versus fake user profile.

3. Gaming Bonus Abuse and Multi-Accounting

Online gaming sites like casinos and betting platforms must be careful when verifying users as actual players, all while offering enticing rewards for new signups (prime targets for fraudsters).

Unfortunately, statistics show that the year 2021 saw a massive 43% surge in online gambling identity theft. A machine learning system here is essential, too, since it can detect poker bots or cheaters much quicker than any human can.

4. BNPL and Account Takeover (ATO Attacks)

These days, Buy Now Pay Later (BNPL) accounts are becoming digital wallets that make online shopping a breeze. But when it comes to fraudsters, they can take advantage of this convenience by stealing login credentials and using them for illegal purchases.

To keep your platform safe, you need to know how users log in – which could vary depending on your market, seasonality, or other factors. The best way is through machine learning algorithms that track the data points at play during authentication processes so you can better protect user accounts.

5. Payment Gateways and Chargeback Fraud

Manually reviewing thousands of transactions quickly isn't feasible. That's why machine learning engines can come in handy here. They act as analytics systems trained to detect fraudulent activities before chargebacks occur.

AI-Powered Credit Scoring and Loan Approval

Lenders are utilizing the power of AI to revolutionize loan approval processes, improve risk assessment, automate document processing, and personalize micro-lending solutions. The credit score is evaluated by taking into account a borrower's history, total income level, work experience, and user behavior. This data is then used to generate an individualized scorecard for each applicant.

ChatGPT could help automate parts of the conversational application process for borrowers. The AI system's contextual knowledge and conversational capabilities could field basic questions from applicants and prompt them for relevant details needed for applications. ChatGPT could potentially assist in explaining loan terms, eligibility requirements, and next steps in the process. This could reduce the workload for human agents and customer service representatives.

Once an application is submitted, ChatGPT's capabilities of natural language processing and statistical analysis could help parse and extract key information from documents like pay stubs, tax returns, bank statements, and credit reports. ChatGPT could potentially flag any inconsistencies, errors, or missing information to ensure complete applications.

However, this traditional method of calculating credit scores still has some serious drawbacks:

- Most calculations are based on historical financial data, which can be difficult for new customers with no borrowing history

- Credit scoring models don't take into consideration new products created specifically for younger audiences

- This doesn't allow banks to get a full view of their customer base, which leads them to open themselves up to errors in their estimations.

Thankfully, machine learning-powered credit scoring systems now offer a more comprehensive way forward - leveraging metrics such as current levels of income, potential earnings capacity, and employment opportunities rather than just relying upon past financial records alone when measuring someone's ability or willingness to pay back debts. These innovative technologies can provide access to finance options previously unavailable by opening doors toward greater inclusion within the increasingly digitized economy.

AI in Loan Approval

The traditional loan approval process can be incredibly time-consuming and laborious. The loan officer must gather all sorts of paperwork, such as government IDs, bank statements, employment proofs, pay stubs, property documents, and any other relevant documents. Then they have to manually verify the important information in each document before sending it off for final review by a manager - which could take days or even weeks.

AI-powered document processing software can make life easier for everyone involved. This tech quickly collects key data from multiple sources at once while also verifying the authenticity of submitted docs. By routing applications through appropriate departments with speed and accuracy, this technology provides customers with an expedited loan approval experience.

AI-Driven Robo-Advisors and Financial Advisory Services

Your financial future is in your own hands. But navigating the rapidly changing world of personal finance can be daunting - that's why technology has come to the rescue! AI-driven robo-advisors are a modern alternative to traditional services, allowing millennials like you to take control of your money with cost-effective and personalized solutions. This new approach is all about making life easier through convenience and customization.

So, say goodbye to stressing over finances. Let tech help you achieve your goals faster.

Robo-advisors powered by Artificial Intelligence are transforming how investors make decisions. They offer lightning-fast analysis capabilities that uncover trends or patterns which may not be very apparent without machine power – giving clients more precise advice on investments while ensuring portfolios remain aligned with one's risk tolerance levels as well as financial objectives for life ahead.

What's more, AI and robo-advisors offer unparalleled convenience for investors on the go. These digital platforms are available 24/7. Thus, users can easily access their accounts or tweak investments any time they like without paying for expensive professional services or waiting for assistance from a traditional advisor.

The sleek user interface also makes it easy even for novices with limited knowledge about finances to start managing their money right away – just another bonus when you're looking into taking control over your own investments.

ChatGPT can be tasked with creating engaging social media posts that inform followers about personal finance topics, engage them with questions, or encourage them to visit your website or read a new blog post.

Some prompts you can use:

- Craft a social media post about tips for saving money

- Create a social media post explaining the basics of investing

- Write a social media post asking followers about their spending habits

- Compose a social media post inquiring about followers' investment choices

- Create a social media post promoting a blog post about reducing debt

These are just examples, you can generate a lot more.

Chapter 4: Unlocking Passive Income Opportunities with AI

The allure of earning money while you sleep, without the constraints of traditional employment, has fueled the desire to explore alternative avenues of generating income. One such avenue that has emerged as a game-changer is the fusion of Artificial Intelligence with passive income opportunities. In this chapter, you will learn about the exciting world of AI-powered passive income, uncovering its potential and how it can be harnessed to unlock new and innovative revenue streams. From investment algorithms and automated trading systems to content creation and digital asset management, this chapter will explore a range of AI-driven strategies that have the power to revolutionize the way you generate income.

Identifying AI Business Opportunities

Currently, organizations can't afford to lag behind when it comes to capitalizing on the potential of AI. But blindly jumping in without a well-thought plan in place could do more harm than good.

To really get the most out of AI – or any technological advancement for that matter – you need an end-game in mind. You need to determine what specifically is going to benefit your company (which may differ from other businesses).

When I help organizations create their own AI strategies, I typically break down the process into two parts:

- First off, take inventory and figure out which possible applications would work best with your particular use case

- Narrow those options down until you're left with only a few top priorities

AI-Enabled Stock Trading and Investment Strategies

When Wall Street statisticians realized they could put AI to use in finance, Anthony Antenucci – the Vice President of Global Business Development at Startek – had this to say to ITPro: "We can now crunch through millions upon millions of data points in real-time and capture insights that our previous models wouldn't be able to detect.". Plus, machine learning has been evolving faster than ever before, making financial institutions one of its earliest adopters.

It's clear that Antenucci isn't the only one who sees the potential in Artificial Intelligence when it comes to trading stocks. Online trading is projected to grow into a $12 billion market by 2028! And like every other industry today, AI will play an integral role as algorithmic trading already accounts for about 60-73% percent of U.S equities, according to recent Wall Street reports.

So how does this tech revolutionize stock markets? Here are some ways Artificial Intelligence is changing things up on Wall Street:

1. Automated Trading

Revolutionized by AI, trading has been completely re-imagined. Algorithms designed to process and analyze massive amounts of data enable automated systems to execute trades with lightning speed - making human traders a thing of the past for those looking for success in the stock market.

AI-driven programs monitor global events and make decisions based on preset rules with a precision that surpasses human capabilities - essential for anyone striving towards their investment goals. So if you want to stay ahead in today's investing world, it's time to get acquainted with this cutting-edge technology.

To use ChatGPT to earn passive income from automated trading, you could use it to develop and refine trading strategies based on the data you provide it.

- **Data Analysis**: Feed the model with relevant financial data and ask it to recognize patterns, correlations, or anomalies. This could be useful for identifying potential investment opportunities.

"Analyze the following stock market data [input data] and identify any notable patterns or trends."

- **Strategy Development**: Task the AI with creating general trading strategies based on certain parameters or market conditions.

"Based on the historical performance of tech stocks during economic downturns, suggest a potential trading strategy."

- **Market News Interpretation**: The model can be used to interpret and summarize financial news, which can be used as part of the decision-making process.

"Summarize the following economic news articles [input articles] and highlight the most important points."

- **Risk Analysis**: You can also ask the AI to provide potential risks associated with a certain investment strategy.

"What are the potential risks of investing heavily in emerging markets?"

2. Sentiment Analysis

Sentiment analysis has become one of the most important aspects in finance, thanks largely due to its ability to provide real-time insights into how people feel about certain stocks or companies through social media posts and news articles – all powered by AI algorithms!

This data allows traders to react faster and make better-informed decisions based on up–to–the–minute market sentiment rather than outdated traditional methods.

As powerful as this technology is, however, there are still challenges related to accuracy. Caution should always be exercised when relying solely on computer-generated predictions during your investment journey.

- **Predictive Analytics**

Gone are the days of relying on guesswork to make investment decisions. With advanced predictive models, savvy stock traders can take advantage of real-time data and spot emerging trends faster than ever before. However, there is still a certain level of risk associated – historical accuracy, market volatility, and external factors all have an effect on these forecasts.

- **Risk Management**

With technology advancing rapidly, investors are now leveraging powerful AI algorithms to identify potential sources of economic instability or company-specific risks that could lead to losses down the line. By taking this extra step in their strategy formulation process, traders have greater chances for success while better equipping themselves against unexpected market shifts - but don't forget that no matter how tech-savvy you may be - investing always carries some degree of risk.

Top Companies Utilizing AI for Smarter Stock Trading

These days, it's no longer a shock that the biggest players in finance have embraced AI to stay ahead of their competition. From BlackRock and Bloomberg to Sentient Technologies, companies around the world are using machine learning algorithms and data analysis tools for more lucrative stock trading. Here's what you need to know:

1. BlackRock

This leading investment management firm has crafted Aladdin, an AI-powered platform created with identifying patterns from big piles of data as well as predicting future market trends in mind.

2. Bloomberg

The financial services powerhouse has constructed its own Artificial Intelligence arsenal called the Bloomberg Terminal, which scans articles, social media posts, and other market info for individualized insights tailored specifically for each user.

3. Sentient Technologies

Specializing in advanced AI applications such as intelligent trading systems, they created their own platform called 'Sentient Investment Management', offering users a suite of sophisticated Machine Learning algorithms aimed at identifying trends in real-time. It has unparalleled accuracy compared to traditional methods used by investors today.

4. Kensho

It's an innovative startup focused on AI solutions, creating tailor-made analytics platforms like Kensho Analytics. It's utilizing ML models able to track down even subtle nuances within huge datasets sourced from multiple mediums, including financial reports and news articles, while predicting how markets will move accordingly. Kensho is allowing traders and investors alike access to valuable resources unavailable before now.

5. Two Sigma Investments

At Two Sigma, a quantitative hedge fund, they're utilizing the power of Artificial Intelligence (AI) to analyze huge amounts of data and build savvy trading strategies. Their platform, Venn, leverages machine learning algorithms to examine information from diverse sources and provide investors with valuable insights.

6. Robinhood

Robinhood is an app-based brokerage service that uses AI to personalize investing for its customers. Its Machine Learning models assess user conduct and supply custom-made investment advice - making it easier than ever before for people to get into the stock market.

Creating ChatGPT Powered Digital Products and Services

Nowadays, AI-driven tools have opened new doors for entrepreneurs to create amazing content and easily launch successful products.

Here are some ideas powered by AI:

1. Create Online Courses

Online courses are more complex than downloadable images or PDFs, but you can still leverage the power of AI to build an online course that will bring in revenue.

ChatGPT can greatly assist in this process by providing content suggestions, automating certain tasks, and offering a unique interactive learning experience.

Here's a step-by-step guide on how you can leverage ChatGPT to create and monetize your online courses:

Step 1: Define Your Course Topic and Objective

Before you start, define the topic and learning objectives of your course. This should be a subject area where you have deep knowledge and expertise. The course objectives should clearly state what students will learn or be able to do after completing the course.

Step 2: Generate Content with ChatGPT

Once you have defined your course topic and objectives, you can use ChatGPT to generate the content. Here's how:

```
Course Outline: Prompt ChatGPT
with "Create a course
for a course on [your topic]".
Use the AI's suggestions as a
starting point and refine where
necessary.

Course Content: Break your topic
down into modules, lessons, and
```

subtopics. For each, you can prompt ChatGPT with "Explain [subtopic] in a simple and understandable way" or "Create a lesson on [subtopic]". This will give you a draft version of your content, which you can edit and refine.

Exercises and Quizzes: You can also use ChatGPT to generate quizzes and exercises for your course. For example, you can prompt it with "Create a quiz on [subtopic]" or "Create an exercise on [subtopic]".

Step 3: Use the Drafts as Basis for your Course Materials

The outputs from ChatGPT are not meant to serve as the final version of your course materials, but they can be a great starting point. Take time to review, edit, and refine the AI-generated content to match your style and meet your course objectives.

Step 4: Build an Interactive Learning Experience

You can use ChatGPT to create a more interactive learning experience for your students. For example, you can integrate ChatGPT into your course platform and use it to provide personalized feedback, answer students' questions, or generate further reading suggestions.

Step 5: Monetize Your Online Course

Once your course is ready, you can monetize it through various methods:

- **Course Sales**: Sell your course on an online learning platform like Udemy, Coursera, or your own website. You can set a fixed price or offer a subscription model.

- **Membership Site**: Create a membership site where students pay a monthly fee to get access to your courses.

- **Consulting or Coaching**: Use your course as a lead magnet for your consulting or coaching services.

- **Affiliate Marketing**: Recommend related products or services in your course and earn affiliate commissions.

Remember, the key to success in online courses is to create high-quality content that genuinely helps your students learn and achieve their goals. Use the power of AI to assist in this process, but always add your personal touch and expertise.

There are plenty of online learning platforms where you can host and sell your courses. Here are a few recommendations:

- **Udemy**: This is one of the most popular online course marketplaces. With Udemy, you don't need to worry about marketing because the platform does it for you. However, you'll have to comply with their pricing structure and they take a significant percentage of your course sales.

- **Teachable**: Teachable allows you to create and sell courses from your own website. It offers powerful course creation tools and allows you to set your own prices. They charge a monthly fee plus a small commission on sales.

- **Coursera**: If you are an educator or affiliated with an educational institution, Coursera is a respected platform for more academic-oriented courses.

- **Thinkific**: Thinkific is similar to Teachable in that it allows you to create, host, and sell courses on your own website. It offers a range of pricing plans and doesn't take a cut of your course sales.

- **Skillshare**: Skillshare is a subscription-based learning platform where students pay a monthly fee for access to all courses. As a teacher, you're paid based on the number of minutes watched in your classes and for every student you refer to Skillshare.

- **Podia**: Podia is a platform that allows you to sell not only online courses but also membership subscriptions and digital downloads. They do not take a percentage of your sales and offer email marketing tools.

- **Kajabi**: Kajabi is an all-in-one platform for creating, hosting, and selling courses. It's more expensive than some other options, but it offers a range of marketing and automation tools in addition to course creation.

- **LearnDash**: If you're using a WordPress website, LearnDash is a powerful LMS (Learning Management System) plugin that allows you to create and sell courses directly from your site.

2. Generate Digital Art through AI

Did you know that there are plenty of Artificial Intelligence image generator tools out there that enable anyone to create stunning artwork? From Midjourney's abstract art pieces to OpenAI's Dall-e creations and Adobe Firefly- whatever type of visuals you need, these apps got your back. If you want cool graphics or images for any project or just want something different than stock photos, give them a try.

3. Produce and Sell Templates

Identify a market that could benefit from ChatGPT templates. This could be small businesses that need customer service bots, bloggers that need content generation, or educators who need automatic grading systems. The potential markets are endless.

4. Create Mockups

With the help of tools like Dall-e and Midjourney, mockup production has never been easier or faster - just enter your design parameters, and voila! You'll have ready-to-use visuals in no time. Whether it's an app concept or packaging layout that needs showcasing, AI mockups are perfect for demonstrating how products will look once they've reached their final form.

5. Design Logos

In addition to mockups, another great option is using AI technology to generate logos. No more relying on graphic designers on Fivver or scouring Etsy - now, you can simply input what colors/objects you want as well as provide examples of what kind of logo aesthetic appeals to you most, and boom: custom designs are generated in seconds! For instance, by utilizing Adobe Firefly's text feature and accessing vector versions of images produced from it, you will have endless customization possibilities when selling these types of digital products online.

6. Create and Sell Stock Music

A more unconventional way of utilizing AI-generated technology is through sound! Companies are always on the hunt for a way to enhance their marketing ads or videos - and they're willing to pay top dollar for it.

With cutting-edge AI capabilities, platforms like Soundraw make creating one-of-a-kind, royalty-free music easy. All you have to do is specify factors like length, tempo, genre, and instrumentation. You will be able to create your own dope tunes that'll be sure to take your content (or any project) up a notch, all without worrying about pesky copyright laws. You can use these tracks yourself in any business endeavor or even sell them off if you really want to maximize profits.

7. Content Creation

Investing in AI-driven production is a win for businesses of any size. The Enterprise Report shows that 94% of professionals consider Artificial Intelligence (AI) an essential tool for success. It's no surprise – this tech can help you and your team produce faster, more accurate work.

Say goodbye to mundane tasks like writing the same piece multiple times or manually sorting through data points. With AI on board, you'll be able to quickly craft top-notch material without spending tons of time on it. Here are some other great benefits:

- **Time-Saving**: Never worry about researching or creating content again; let AI do the work!

- **Cost-Effective**: Get more done by producing quality output with fewer resources.

- **Format Versatility**: Generate different types of content (blogs, articles, etc.) without breaking a sweat.

- **Consistent Quality**: Great results each time as long as the input is accurate.

- **Unlimited Scalability**: Quickly and efficiently create millions upon millions of words thanks to automation.

Here are some ways you can use ChatGPT for content creation:

1. Blog Posts and Articles

ChatGPT can help you draft blog posts or articles on a variety of topics. Provide the model with the topic and some key points you want to cover, and it will generate a detailed, coherent text.

```
Input:
```

```
{ "title": "The Future of AI",
"points": ["Current state of
AI", "Potential future
developments", "Ethical
considerations"] }
```

```
Output:
```

```
(Article text)
```

2. Social Media Posts

ChatGPT can generate engaging social media posts. Insert the type of post, platform, and main idea, and it will create a suitable update.

```
Input:
```

```
{ "post_type": "Twitter",
"main_idea": "Promoting a new
blog post about AI" }
```

```
Output:
```

```
"Excited to share our latest
blog post exploring the
intriguing world of AI! Dive
into the current state of AI,
potential future advances, and
the ethical questions we should
```

```
all be asking. #AI #FutureTech
(link)"
```

3. Writing Prompts and Story Generation

ChatGPT can create interesting writing prompts or even generate short stories based on a given prompt.

```
Input:

{ "prompt": "A world where AI
has become self-aware" }

Output:

(Short story text)
```

4. Poetry

ChatGPT can create poems on a given theme or in a specific style.

```
Input:

{ "theme": "Autumn", "style":
"Haiku" }

Output:

"Leaves falling softly,

Autumn's breath in the cool air,
```

```
Nature's art on display."
```

Personalizing Content for Your Audience

Creating a powerful message that speaks to your audience is essential in order to drive engagement and build lasting relationships. To get the most out of it, take some time to understand who you're speaking with - their needs wants, and expectations. Leverage AI technology for content tailored specifically towards them, using customer data, if possible, for even more personalization.

If broad reach is what you're after, make sure you generate content in multiple languages. When crafting your message from scratch, there's no better way than to take advantage of all available resources. When done right, it'll speak directly to people's hearts.

AI in Real Estate

AI is revolutionizing the real estate game - transforming how appraisers, mortgage lenders, and developers go about their work. Here are four ways this tech is impacting the property industry:

1. Offering Personalized Advice to Customers

The recommendation engine used by e-commerce giants such as Amazon? It now extends far beyond retail - allowing gargantuan estate agents with hundreds or even thousands of properties on offer to save customers a ton of time by refining their offerings and improving targeting accuracy. AI can craft customized listings for clients based on what they want from a property in addition to previous viewings. It can even use profiling techniques to give first-time buyers relevant offers based on their demographic attributes or preferences, which have worked well for other customers in similar situations before them – saving everyone from having to manually sift through ever-growing databases.

2. Analyzing the Market with AI

Investing in real estate can be a huge gamble, and having the ability to predict market trends is crucial. AI has stepped onto the scene with powerful tools for investors to estimate sale or rent prices, observe patterns starting to form, and identify unique investments - all while keeping their risk low.

This cutting-edge technology works by combining human expertise and data analysis from various sources, thus allowing for more informed decisions when it comes time to invest your hard-earned money into potential profit streams. AI allows you to see beyond what's available today – making predictions on future events that could have significant impacts on both short-term gains as well as long-term returns. It's no surprise then why savvy entrepreneurs are turning towards these predictive models for their investments - they provide an opportunity quite unlike any other.

3. Simplifies Customer Care

No one enjoys being put on hold and playing phone tag. The fast-paced lifestyle people lead make it difficult for customer care to keep up. For small real estate agents, hiring staff for an around-the-clock call center simply isn't feasible - or even necessary. AI chatbots excel at handling most inquiries, often outperforming agents when suggesting properties.

Plus, with advancements in natural language processing and machine learning technology, you can now interact with them like you would any other person. So don't sweat; just let the bots take over your customer service woes so you can focus on bigger things. Recently, I subscribed to a service by mistake. I contacted them for a refund and I was surprised at how quickly their chatbot managed it and sent me my refund.

4. Smart Contracts

Some organizations don't take blockchain lightly. It's important to understand that the rapid growth of smart contracts will revolutionize data-driven transactions and provide businesses with unprecedented opportunities for success.

Real estate deals can be streamlined by these secure contracts - providing a hassle-free way to guarantee accuracy without any human involvement. Imagine being able to purchase real estate as conveniently as you would buy something online - that's looking more likely every day.

Say goodbye to the days of slaving over paperwork and hello to the new era of smart contracts. Cut out all risks associated with clerical errors or fraud. These pre-defined terms ensure your transactions are airtight from beginning to end. Let technology do its thing - no more worrying about sketchy deals or going back and forth on documents. Smart contracts make sure everything is taken care of accurately and securely, so you can kick back without a care in the world.

5. Startups and AI

As tech titans like Google, Amazon, Apple, and Microsoft stake their claim in the AI revolution, it's no surprise that this cutting-edge technology is becoming more commonplace. From conversing with Siri and Alexa to automated robots for customer service analytics or self-driving cars on the roads - these technological advances are laying the ground for an intelligent future.

McKinsey Global Survey data from 2017–2022 shows how far this has come: adoption of Artificial Intelligence has skyrocketed over recent years!

With such rapid progress being made towards smarter systems and service improvements across industries such as banking and finance, cyber security protection, or content creation, now is the time to embrace all that AI can offer.

Freelancing and AI

As the AI sector continues to explode, skilling up is becoming ever-more essential for those wanting to take advantage of this disruptive technology. In just two years, from 2015-2017, LinkedIn's required skills for AI-based jobs increased by 190%.

According to Grand View Research's latest figures, AI is predicted to hit a massive $997.8 billion market size in 2028. Getting ahead now will be key to success in the future.

But how can you get your foot in the door?

1. Join Kaggle Competitions

Kaggle is the ultimate data science hub - boasting powerful tools and resources to help you reach your goals. It's not only a financial resource for most aspiring data scientists, but it also serves as an invaluable learning platform where you can hone skills, acquire knowledge, sharpen abilities, and even learn from mistakes by submitting code. Plus, regular practice keeps those skills sharpened.

2. Boost Your Digital Credibility

In a world of work dominated by digital technology, it's crucial to have an impressive online presence - employers are often scouting for potential employees based on their portfolios or posts they've shared in the past. Keep your resume and profile up-to-date with relevant job experience/projects as well as stay informed about emerging trends within AI; this will demonstrate to others that you're knowledgeable of what's going on in the industry.

3. Launch into Freelance Marketplaces

Artificial Intelligence is an exciting field for graduates and individuals who want to make extra money. If you want to start earning cash right away, plenty of businesses also offer freelance gigs related to AI. Be smart when picking out jobs so you don't get caught up in bidding wars; don't be scared to take risks along the way.

4. ChatGPT

ChatGPT is revolutionizing the way people work. This language model has all you need to get ahead and make money. With its advanced capabilities, you can:

- Write blogs and articles
- Write code in any language needed
- Rapidly and accurately translate texts

- Generate engaging content ideas for marketing purposes

- Lightning-fast support response times

How to Create Blogs and Articles Using ChatGPT:

Step 1: Define your topic and gather initial research. Begin by choosing a specific topic or subject for your blog post or article.

Step 2: Familiarize yourself with ChatGPT. Take some time to familiarize yourself with ChatGPT and understand its capabilities. This will help you leverage its strengths effectively during the writing process. ChatGPT is a powerful language model that can generate human-like text, but it's important to review and edit the output for accuracy and coherence.

Step 3: Access the ChatGPT interface. You can access it through the OpenAI platform or directly use the API. Choose the option that best suits your needs and budget. If you're using the OpenAI platform, log in to your account and navigate to the ChatGPT interface.

Step 4: Craft an engaging introduction. Begin by writing an engaging introduction to capture the reader's attention. Provide a brief overview of the topic and why it is relevant or interesting. Consider using a hook or a compelling question to draw readers in.

Step 5: Start the conversation with ChatGPT. Enter the initial prompt or question in the ChatGPT interface. Clearly communicate your objective to ChatGPT, such as "Help me write an article about [your topic]. Provide an outline and some key points to cover."

Step 6: Collaborate with ChatGPT. Engage in a conversation with ChatGPT, asking for specific information, examples, or arguments related to your topic. Ask open-ended questions to encourage detailed responses. For example, "Can you provide some statistics or studies that support this point?" or "What are the counterarguments to this perspective?"

Step 7: Review and refine the generated content. As ChatGPT generates responses, carefully review the output. Keep in mind that the model may occasionally produce inaccurate or nonsensical information. Edit and refine the text to ensure accuracy, coherence, and readability. You may need to ask follow-up questions or request clarifications to enhance the quality of the responses.

Step 8: Structure your content. Organize the information provided by ChatGPT into a logical structure. Create headings, subheadings, and bullet points to outline your main arguments or sections. This will make it easier to arrange the content and maintain a coherent flow throughout the article.

Step 9: Add your personal touch. Although ChatGPT provides valuable information, you need to add your unique perspective and voice to the content. Incorporate your own thoughts, experiences, and insights into the article. This will give it a personal touch and make it more engaging for readers.

Step 10: Edit and polish your article. After incorporating the generated content into your article, thoroughly review and edit the entire piece. Check for grammar, spelling, and punctuation errors. Make sure that the content is well-structured and flows smoothly. Trim any unnecessary or repetitive information. Make sure your writing is clear, concise, and compelling.

Step 11: Fact-check and cite sources. Double-check all the information provided in the article for accuracy. If you've used specific statistics, studies, or references from ChatGPT, fact-check them and ensure they are from reliable sources and not something it made up. Cite your sources properly to give credit and provide additional credibility to your content.

Step 12: Proofread and finalize. Before publishing or sharing your article, proofread it one final time.

Read it aloud to catch any errors or awkward phrasing. Pay attention to formatting, headings, and overall readability. Make any necessary adjustments to create a polished and professional final draft.

By following these steps, you can effectively leverage ChatGPT to assist you in generating content for blog posts and articles. Remember that while ChatGPT can provide valuable insights, it's important to review and edit the output to meet your specific needs and standards.

How to Generate Ideas for Marketing Purposes Using ChatGPT:

Step 1: Define your marketing goals and target audience. Start by clearly defining your marketing goals. Determine what you aim to achieve, such as increasing brand awareness, driving sales, or improving customer engagement. Identify your target audience, their demographics, preferences, and pain points. This will help you tailor your generated ideas to resonate with your audience.

Step 2: Access the ChatGPT interface. Log in to the OpenAI platform or use the ChatGPT API directly, depending on your preference and access. If you're using the OpenAI platform, navigate to the ChatGPT interface.

Step 3: Familiarize yourself with ChatGPT. Take some time to understand the capabilities of

ChatGPT. Explore its strengths in generating creative ideas and brainstorming. Keep in mind that ChatGPT is a language model that may provide a range of suggestions, so reviewing and selecting the most relevant and feasible ideas is important.

Step 4: Craft a clear prompt. Compose a clear and concise prompt for ChatGPT. Clearly communicate your objective, such as "Generate marketing ideas to increase brand awareness among millennials" or "Brainstorm creative strategies for launching a new product in the tech industry."

Step 5: Engage in a conversation with ChatGPT. Initiate a conversation with ChatGPT by providing your prompt. Ask open-ended questions to stimulate idea generation. For example, "What are some unique marketing approaches that have proven successful in the past?" or "How can we leverage social media to reach a wider audience?"

Step 6: Collaborate and explore ideas. As ChatGPT generates responses, review the ideas presented. Collaborate with ChatGPT by asking for specific examples, case studies, or strategies related to your marketing goals. Encourage ChatGPT to provide detailed insights and rationale behind the suggested ideas.

Step 7: Evaluate and refine the generated ideas. Evaluate the generated ideas based on their relevance, feasibility, and alignment with your marketing goals and target audience. Identify the most promising concepts and refine them to fit your specific needs. Consider combining or modifying ideas to create unique and innovative approaches.

Step 8: Prioritize the generated ideas based on their potential impact and feasibility. Create a list or spreadsheet to organize the ideas, categorize them by marketing channels or tactics, and assign priority levels. This will help you develop a comprehensive marketing strategy.

Step 9: Expand on the ideas. Use the generated ideas as a starting point and expand on them. Add more details, supporting arguments, and action steps to turn them into actionable marketing plans. Consider potential challenges, risks, and mitigation strategies for each idea.

Step 10: Validate and test the ideas. Before implementing the ideas, consider conducting market research or seeking feedback from your target audience. Validate the concepts by conducting surveys, focus groups, or A/B testing to gauge their potential effectiveness. Refine the ideas based on the feedback received.

Step 11: Develop an integrated marketing strategy. Based on the generated ideas and their validation, develop an integrated marketing strategy that incorporates multiple channels and tactics. Align the ideas with your overall brand messaging and ensure consistency across all marketing touchpoints.

Step 12: Execute, monitor, and iterate. Implement your marketing strategy and closely monitor its performance. Track key metrics and indicators to measure the effectiveness of each idea. Analyze the results and iterate on the strategy based on the insights gained. Continuously refine and optimize your marketing efforts.

By following these steps, you can effectively utilize ChatGPT to generate ideas for marketing purposes. Remember to review, refine, and tailor the ideas generated by ChatGPT to align with your specific marketing goals, target audience, and brand identity. ChatGPT can serve as a valuable tool in brainstorming and creative ideation, but human expertise and judgment are crucial in selecting and executing the most effective strategies.

Ready to take advantage of this innovative tool? There are a lot more opportunities out there to turn a profit using ChatGPT, including:

1. Start Your Freelance Copywriting Business

This handy writing assistant allows marketers access to website copy, landing pages, social media posts, or blog entries – all written at lightning speed! Plus, it can write emails and proposals when communicating with potential clients.

2. Create and Sell Chatbot Applications

Create customized chatbots utilizing ChatGPT's powerful technology, then license or outright sell them off as virtual assistants, customer service representatives, etc. You never know who might want one (or more) – so get started now!

3. Create and Sell Videos with ChatGPT

As a content creator or SEO pro, ChatGPT can elevate your video projects to the next level. Its text-to-speech plugins make creating captivating voiceovers for videos an easy feat.

You can then sell these videos. Plus, use it to optimize YouTube descriptions with up-to-date SEO strategies - offering this alongside your services as an expert in this field is sure to set you apart from competitors.

4. Self-Publish eBooks

ChatGPT makes it easy for anyone who wants to self-publish eBooks and monetize their writing skills. Generate income through subscriptions or selling access without having any coding knowledge whatsoever. Every sentence crafted speaks volumes - so why not put all of those words into action?

AI-Driven Marketplaces and Gig Platforms

The gig lifestyle is no different than contract or freelance work. Essentially, the term "gig" describes how individuals make money through digital platforms.

This economy consists of a wide variety of professionals with distinct skill sets and talents. Gig workers can be either freelancers or independent contractors - some apps are solely for certain professions offering specific services, while others welcome any type of worker with diverse abilities.

Currently, people have embraced creative ways to generate income. Whether you're an artist trying to sell your art online or someone who works remotely as a consultant, something out there fits your skillset. With so many resources available now at your fingertips, earning cash from home has never been easier.

12 Best Gig Economy Platforms to Look Into

1. Prospa: The gold standard for finding profitable side hustles

2. Fiverr: A great way to monetize your skills

3. Upwork: Perfect if you want flexible work with top-notch clients

4. Appen: Take on gigs from the comfort of your own home

5. Crowdspring: An online marketplace connecting creative professionals with businesses, startups, and entrepreneurs in need of design solutions.

6. Tongal: Offers users access to thousands of projects needing assistance

7. Toptal: A platform that enables companies around the world to hire freelancers

8. 99designs: Accessible portfolio website where customers can find new talent

9. Freelancer: Another freelancing platform with a wide variety of jobs

10. Contently: Helps freelancers showcase their work experience

11. FreelanceDiary: A job board just for freelance creatives.

12. PeoplePerHour: Connects employers and potential employees

Generating Passive Income with AI-Powered Affiliate Marketing

Now, let me tell you about another way to earn passive income. It is quite easy compared to the previous ones. Whether you're a budding entrepreneur or an experienced businessperson, you can leverage cutting-edge tech and cash in on the rewards. Look into products, tools, and services related to your niche that use Artificial Intelligence – then join their affiliate programs for unique links. Use these links to promote offerings through your website, blog, or social media channels. Every successful sale is money in the bank! Get ahead of the competition by embracing AI advancements – be a 21st-century mogul and watch those profits pile up!

Chapter 5: Applications for Profitable Ventures

This chapter delves into the realm of applications for profitable ventures, exploring a diverse range of industries and strategies that can pave the way for success. From innovative technologies and disruptive business models to sustainable practices and global market expansion, this chapter uncovers the key elements contributing to modern enterprises' profitability. Whether you are an aspiring entrepreneur or a seasoned business professional, the insights shared within these pages will empower you to navigate the competitive business landscape and unlock new avenues for financial growth.

Leveraging AI in Financial Services

The cutthroat financial services industry (FSI) is a bloody battlefield with stringent rules. To stay ahead of the competition, companies need to get creative and employ cutting-edge tech - like AI - that analyzes past data sets to forecast future events and enrich customer experiences. AI has become an absolute must in this arena if businesses want to stand out from their rivals. So, if you're looking for your business model to remain at the top of the food chain amongst fierce competitors, you've got to think outside the box and find innovative ways to utilize technology.

AI-Driven Marketing

AI's application in marketing may seem like something out of sci-fi movies, but it's already here! According to Salesforce stats, only 29% of marketers used AI back in 2018. However, this number skyrocketed by 84% by 2020 - proving its undeniable potential as an effective tool for success.

Content Marketing

Content is the heartbeat of any successful marketing strategy. With AI advancements, crafting content that speaks to our target market and generates real results is simpler than ever. Take Buzzfeed, for example - they've become a prime model on how Artificial Intelligence can be used to upgrade their operations for massive success. From predicting which posts will go viral, customizing user experiences, automating keyword selection and categorization, all the way through personalizing each visitor's experience with tailored content.

But beyond just using AI tools in building your content plan, there are other aspects too:

- What type of material should you create?

- Where should you post it?

- How often do you release new pieces?
- And what kind of tone or form fits best with your message?

All these questions have something crucial in common. They need precise consideration before making decisions that could sway the future direction of your brand and business growth. After all, when it comes down to creating a lasting impact online, content is king.

Given a prompt, ChatGPT can generate human-like text that's coherent and contextually relevant. Remember to review and edit the content to ensure it aligns with your brand voice and content strategy.

```
Input: "Write a blog post about
the benefits of plant-based
diets."

Output: "[Draft of a blog post]"
```

If you're stuck for content ideas, ChatGPT can help. Provide it with a topic or theme, and it can generate a list of content ideas or titles.

```
Input: "Generate content ideas
for a gardening blog."

Output: "[List of content
ideas]"
```

ChatGPT can help optimize your content for SEO. It can suggest keywords, draft meta descriptions, or generate SEO-friendly headlines based on your input.

```
Input: "Create an SEO-friendly
headline for a blog post about
cryptocurrency trends."

Output: "5 Key Cryptocurrency
Trends of 2023: A Comprehensive
Guide"
```

ChatGPT can draft emails for your marketing campaigns. It can help with creating engaging subject lines, drafting the body of the email, or crafting CTAs.

```
Input: "Write a promotional
email for our new product
launch."

Output: "[Draft of a promotional
email]"
```

From creating engaging posts to drafting responses for customer comments, ChatGPT can assist with managing your social media presence.

```
Input: "Write a response to a
customer who had a positive
experience with our product."
```

```
Output: "We're so glad to hear
you had a great experience with
our product! Thank you for the
feedback."
```

Public Relations

Public relations has undergone a major transformation in the age of social media and digital influencers—and AI can help you keep up. You need to know which content creators, sponsored or unsponsored, are best aligned with your brand's values and appeal—so why not let technology do some of the work?

AI-powered platforms have made it possible to match products with people with an audience most likely to relate to them. Taking this even further is innovative chatbot tech like Lil Miquela, a totally virtual persona with millions of followers worldwide! Brands such as Calvin Klein and Prada pay her hefty fees for her influence, thanks to her highly engaged fan base.

But beyond finding influencers, Artificial Intelligence can also support other PR tasks like crafting press releases, optimizing external messages for maximum visibility across all channels (digital or otherwise), and researching ideal outlets for coverage opportunities. All these things require effort, but AI makes them much easier.

Advertising

Advertisers face the challenge of optimizing ad placements to ensure they deliver maximum value. To do this successfully, leveraging AI-driven advertising tools and platforms is important. Facebook and Google are at the forefront in terms of online marketing capabilities; both offer powerful features that use audience segmentation combined with predictive analytics.

Segmentation divides people into distinct groups based on characteristics like age, gender, income level, or interests – among other criteria – while predictive analytics indicate which audiences would be most receptive to particular products or services. Advertisers can then target select customers with multiple variations of their ads for testing purposes. It is a process made much simpler compared to traditional methods such as TV commercials or print publications, where it's often difficult to determine whether sales were driven by effective advertisement placement or external factors.

For ultimate success, though, these AI-powered solutions should be incorporated as part of an overall strategic plan incorporating all aspects of digital marketing - from content creation through optimization techniques and beyond.

AI-Powered Chatbots and Virtual

Assistants

Chatbots are advanced applications that interact with customers in a realistic way, be it through text or audio. Their primary role is to guide users by providing instructions on how to complete tasks as well as supplying helpful info such as contact details and product information. Chatbots can also arrange calendar appointments, connect to knowledge bases for real-time support, and access self-service portals - making them invaluable tools for customer service departments. In short, chatbot technology bridges the gap between humans and computers with their AI capabilities, allowing businesses to interact with customers quickly while staying engaged in conversations at all times.

These days, virtual assistants are the go-to for all the mundane tasks that take up so much time. From Amazon Alexa to Apple Siri and Google Assistant, these personal software agents are here to simplify life. They can check bookings, set alarms, make calls, or type messages as if they were a real human assistant! They even offer personalized solutions with troubleshooting in an almost conversational manner. Plus, Alexa has advanced features which help develop voice chatbots — perfect for times when you just want someone to talk it out with! Don't let tedious daily tasks weigh you down - there's a virtual buddy ready and willing to lend a helping hand.

You're probably wondering why you should invest in a virtual assistant or chatbot. Having these digital tools can help your business in more ways than one, from boosted productivity to top-notch customer service. Here's what sets them apart:

The Advantages of Investing in Voice Assistants

1. **Maximum Productivity**: With voice assistance software, doing things takes less time and effort, so you don't have to take breaks while multitasking - perfect for busy adults who need an extra hand (or two).

2. **No More Navigation Woes**: If you ever find yourself on unfamiliar roads, voice assistants will be there to guide the way with their seamless navigation abilities. Plus, they make road trips even better by offering some great entertainment options along the way.

3. **Unparalleled Organization**: Many people love utilizing their voice assistant when it comes to organize their schedule, stay up-to-date with news headlines, check weather conditions, and even create shopping lists.

4. **Increased Privacy Controls**: With better access due to the convenience of voice

commands compared to typing things out manually, plus advanced security features that allow users an extra layer of safety from unwanted intrusions into personal information, making sure each user's private data stays safe and secure has never been simpler thanks technology giants like Amazon Alexa and Google Home respectively.

5. **Seamless User Experience**: Last but not least, integrating a virtual helper into one's day-to-day lifestyle offers unbeatable advantages when it comes to providing tailor-made recommendations based upon individualized preferences, which truly takes a carefree living experience next level.

Benefits of Chatbot Technology

Chatbots have become a major asset for businesses in today's digital world. They can be used to do everything from providing information about products and services, helping customers shop online, setting reminders, creating polls and surveys - the list goes on! Here are some of the key advantages that come with utilizing chatbot technology:

1. Finding what you need is very quick with chatbots. They'll help you get answers quickly compared to searching manually.

2. AI-powered bots can understand multiple languages, so no matter where your customer base is located, everyone will receive accurate info right away without having language barriers get in their way.

3. Automating processes means more efficiency and less time spent waiting around – perfect for busy people who want results fast.

4. Customers won't have trouble finding solutions with omnichannel support like co-browsing capabilities and video chatting options available across all channels.

AI for Trends Prediction

The age of human-machine collaboration is here, and I wanted to know what ChatGPT was most excited about when it comes to the 2023 AI trends. So, I posed five questions – each aimed at uncovering the biggest accomplishments in 2022 and any fads that should be put to rest the next year, all while exploring ways for leaders to leverage AI without too much effort or money.

Keep in mind that the answers were all prefaced by the model stating that it only has knowledge up until September 2021. Here's what it said:

What is the greatest advancement in Artificial Intelligence this past year?

"One notable advancement in recent years has been the development and implementation of GPT-3, the model on which I am based. GPT-3 (Generative Pre-trained Transformer 3) is a highly advanced language model capable of understanding and generating human-like text. Its ability to perform various language-related tasks, such as translation, summarization, question answering, and more, has shown great promise in the field of natural language processing.

Additionally, breakthroughs have been made in the application of AI to computer vision tasks. Convolutional Neural Networks (CNNs) have revolutionized image recognition and object detection, enabling AI systems to achieve remarkable accuracy in tasks like image classification and object recognition. Generative models such as Generative Adversarial Networks (GANs) have also contributed to generating realistic images and videos.

Advancements have also been made in AI applications across various industries, including healthcare, finance, autonomous vehicles, and robotics. AI is being utilized to improve medical diagnostics, develop more efficient trading algorithms, enhance self-driving cars' capabilities, and enable robots to perform complex tasks."

What's one trend you can't wait for us to experience in 2023?

"One trend that has been gaining momentum and is highly anticipated is the continued development and adoption of augmented reality (AR) and virtual reality (VR) technologies. AR and VR have the potential to transform various aspects of our lives, including entertainment, gaming, education, training, and communication.

In 2023, we can expect to see advancements in AR and VR hardware, software, and content, making these technologies more immersive, realistic, and accessible. This may include improvements in headsets, controllers, haptic feedback systems, and the development of more sophisticated and interactive virtual environments.

AR and VR have the potential to revolutionize entertainment and gaming by providing immersive and interactive experiences. They can also enhance education and training by creating virtual simulations and scenarios that enable hands-on learning and skill development. Additionally, AR and VR can enable new forms of communication and collaboration, allowing people to interact in virtual spaces regardless of their physical location.

Overall, the trend of AR and VR development in 2023 holds the promise of expanding our horizons, creating new experiences, and pushing the boundaries of what is possible in the realm of digital technology."

What are some of the most overhyped techs in recent years?

"While it's subjective to some extent, there are a few technologies that have garnered significant attention and hype but may not have lived up to their full potential or practical applications. Here are a few examples:

Blockchain Technology: Blockchain technology gained immense popularity with the rise of cryptocurrencies like Bitcoin. While blockchain technology has its merits in terms of decentralized and secure transactions, the hype surrounding it often overshadows its limitations and practicality for many use cases. It's important to assess whether blockchain is truly necessary for a given application before implementing it.

Internet of Things (IoT): The Internet of Things, which refers to the interconnection of everyday objects with the Internet, has been hyped as a game-changer in various domains, including home automation, healthcare, and industrial applications. However, the widespread adoption and practical implementation of IoT devices have been slower than initially anticipated. Challenges related to security, interoperability, and privacy need to be addressed for IoT to reach its full potential.

3D Printing: Also known as additive manufacturing, 3D printing has been hailed as a revolutionary technology with the potential to transform manufacturing, prototyping, and personalized production. While 3D printing has made significant advancements and found valuable applications in certain industries, its widespread adoption and impact on traditional manufacturing processes have been more limited than initially expected.

It's important to note that while these technologies may not have met all the initial hype, they still hold value and continue to evolve. They may find more practical applications or be combined with other emerging technologies to unlock their full potential in the future. Evaluating the practicality, scalability, and real-world applications of technology is crucial to avoid unwarranted hype and ensure meaningful progress."

How can decision-makers get the most value out of AI with minimal resources and time invested?

"To get value out of AI with minimal resources and time invested, decision-makers can consider the following strategies:

Define Clear Objectives: Clearly define the problem or opportunity you want to address with AI. Focus on specific areas where AI can provide the most value and align with your business objectives. This clarity helps in efficient resource allocation and reduces unnecessary investment in unrelated AI initiatives.

Leverage Existing Resources: Assess your existing data and technology infrastructure. You may already have valuable data that can be leveraged for AI applications. Look for opportunities to repurpose existing tools, frameworks, or platforms to minimize costs and implementation time.

Start Small and Scale Gradually: Instead of attempting large-scale AI projects right away, start with small, manageable pilots or proof-of-concept projects. This approach allows you to validate the effectiveness of AI applications in your specific context and identify any challenges or limitations early on. Once successful, you can gradually scale up the AI initiatives.

Collaborate and Partner: Seek collaborations or partnerships with AI experts, research institutions, or technology vendors who can provide guidance, expertise, or pre-existing AI models and solutions. This can save time and resources by leveraging their knowledge and experience.

Emphasize Data Quality and Preparation: AI models heavily rely on high-quality and well-prepared data. Invest time in data cleaning, preprocessing, and augmentation to ensure the best possible input for AI algorithms. This can lead to improved performance and accuracy of AI applications.

Explore Open-Source Solutions: Open-source AI frameworks and tools, such as TensorFlow and PyTorch, offer a cost-effective way to leverage AI capabilities. These resources provide pre-built models, tutorials, and a supportive community, making it easier to implement AI solutions with limited resources.

Consider Cloud-Based AI Services: Cloud providers offer AI services that allow organizations to access AI capabilities without significant upfront infrastructure costs. These services provide pre-trained models, APIs, and scalable computing resources, making AI implementation more accessible and cost-effective.

Invest in AI Talent: Building internal AI capabilities may require additional investment but can lead to long-term value. Recruit or train employees with the necessary AI skills to maximize the value extracted from AI initiatives. Additionally, leveraging AI consultants or experts for short-term engagements can provide valuable guidance and accelerate progress.

By following these strategies, decision-makers can start realizing the value of AI with limited resources and time, allowing for gradual and efficient adoption of AI technologies aligned with their specific needs and constraints."

Is there something they must stop doing today if benefits are to be expected tomorrow?

"If decision-makers want to maximize the benefits of AI in the future, there are a few things they should consider stopping or avoiding:

Ignoring Data Quality: Decision-makers must prioritize data quality. Relying on poor-quality data can lead to inaccurate or biased AI models and hinder the effectiveness of AI applications. It is crucial to invest in data quality control, data governance, and data management practices to ensure the reliability and integrity of the data used for AI.

Focusing Solely on Short-Term Gains: While it's important to see tangible benefits from AI in the short term, decision-makers should avoid a myopic approach that neglects long-term strategies. AI initiatives often require iterative development, experimentation, and continuous learning. By prioritizing long-term goals and investments, decision-makers can create sustainable AI strategies that yield lasting benefits.

Overlooking Ethical Considerations: Ethical implications are crucial when implementing AI technologies. Decision-makers must actively address potential biases, privacy concerns, and algorithmic fairness. By integrating ethical considerations into the AI development process and implementing transparent and responsible AI practices, organizations can build trust, mitigate risks, and ensure the long-term benefits of AI.

Neglecting Human Expertise and Collaboration: AI should not replace human expertise but complement it. Decision-makers should recognize that AI is a tool to augment human capabilities and enable collaboration between humans and machines. Encouraging interdisciplinary teams, fostering a culture of collaboration, and promoting knowledge sharing between domain experts and AI specialists can lead to more effective and valuable AI applications.

Disregarding Continuous Learning and Adaptation: AI technologies evolve rapidly, and decision-makers should embrace a mindset of continuous learning and adaptation. Staying informed about the latest advancements, industry trends, and best practices in AI is crucial to make informed decisions, identifying emerging opportunities, and remaining competitive in an AI-driven landscape.

By stopping or avoiding these practices, decision-makers can create a foundation that enables the future benefits of AI. It involves nurturing a data-driven and ethically conscious approach, focusing on long-term strategies, fostering collaboration, and embracing a culture of continuous learning and adaptation."

AI-Driven Fraud Detection and Risk Management

With machines having an easier time processing huge datasets than humans, slicing and dicing through information has never been simpler. Your team can now take advantage of these benefits:

1. **Swift Detection**: When it comes to uncovering patterns or suspicious behavior, AI-driven systems are light-years ahead – what would have taken months for agents to detect is quickly identified by machine learning algorithms.

2. **Faster Reviews**: Let automation do the heavy lifting when combing through data

points so your human team can focus on other tasks rather than spend time manually reviewing information themselves.

3. **Accurate Predictions at Scale**: As you feed more data into ML engines, they become better trained and learn how to identify trends that may be too complex for humans alone to find in large datasets.

4. **Cost-Effective Solution**: No need for additional personnel if you've got a top-notch machine handling all the info. Whether there's a lot or only little incoming activity throughout the year, this system will reduce risk management costs without sacrificing efficiency.

Last but not least, algorithms don't need to recharge. They stay on the clock 24/7 to detect fraud. No matter how hardworking your team of fraud managers is, Monday mornings can still be overwhelming with the manual reviews that piled up over the weekend.

Luckily, machine learning algorithms can lighten the load by sifting through obviously fraudulent or acceptable cases — research from computer scientists at the University of Jakarta has proven that these AI-driven systems are as accurate as 96% when it comes to fighting e-commerce scams!

AI in Healthcare

AI and machine learning are revolutionizing healthcare. Health organizations have stockpiled massive amounts of data, ranging from medical records to population information, claims info, and clinical trial details.

AI-enabled technologies can go through all this data swiftly and discover patterns that would elude the human eye. Deep learning algorithms leverage these insights to help health firms make more informed business decisions as well as better patient care experiences.

Studies show that AI may even outshine humans in some key areas like disease diagnosis - for example, it's already outperforming radiologists when detecting cancerous growths or helping scientists build cohorts for costly clinical trials with ease.

Benefits of AI in Healthcare

1. Revolutionizing User Experiences

With the help of large datasets and advanced machine learning, healthcare systems can output more accurate insights, leading to improved satisfaction both internally and externally.

2. Optimizing Operational Efficiency

By using AI tech to uncover data patterns, organizations are able to maximize their resources which leads to an increase in efficiency for clinical processes/workflows and financial operations.

3. Connecting Diverse Health Data

It's not uncommon for healthcare information to be found on different platforms with various formats. Thanks to Artificial Intelligence and ML techniques, companies can combine this scattered data into a unified view that focuses on people instead of numbers.

AI in Healthcare Use Case: Natural Language Processing

When subject matter experts collaborate with AI algorithms to detect and sort data patterns representing real-world language use in the healthcare sector, they enable natural language processing (NLP). This allows decision-makers to quickly access relevant information and make informed care or business decisions.

Healthcare Payers

With NLP power, health plans can deploy virtual agents using conversational AI to give members personalized answers on demand.

Government Health Professionals

Caseworkers can leverage AI services for rapid assessment of case notes to better support their clients' needs.

Clinical Operations and Data Managers

Clinical trial managers can accelerate searches and medical coding validation through Artificial Intelligence solutions - reducing the time needed for study initiation/amendment/management.

How AI Is Transforming Healthcare and Streamlining Clinical Decisions

Gone are the days of doctors spending hours looking through medical literature for answers. With modern machine learning tech and biomedical data, clinicians can quickly access information backed by experts in the field thanks to electronic health records.

AI-powered clinical decision support systems with natural language processing capabilities provide fast responses to questions posed like you would a colleague in everyday conversation - no more stilted technical jargon. It's not just about speed either; these solutions deliver accurate information so that healthcare professionals have peace of mind when providing patient-centered care.

Chapter 6: Balancing Progress with Humanity

This chapter will go into explaining the relationship between technological progress and preserving humanity. In this chapter, you will get a deeper understanding of the ethical and social dimensions of Artificial Intelligence (AI), guiding you in the responsible utilization of this powerful tool.

Addressing Fairness and Bias in AI Systems

In the age of Artificial Intelligence, ML algorithms can offer incredible insights - when applied with non-biased data, of course. Unfortunately, many AI models are prone to prejudice that is often ingrained in their training datasets due to social disparities.

For instance, Amazon's 2018 recruitment tool was found guilty of giving male applicants an unfair advantage over female candidates and punishing resumes including terms associated with femininity (such as "women's or feminine"). Therefore, we must strive for fairness and challenge bias when engineering machine learning systems.

To tackle this challenge successfully, a range of considerations must be taken into account:

Data Bias: It's no secret that AI models can discriminate if the training datasets they draw from are biased. So, it's key for developers to make sure whatever data is being used accurately represents reality - free of any hidden prejudices. Otherwise, you might as well be setting yourself up for failure.

Algorithmic Transparency: Complex deep neural networks may lack transparency, making it difficult for engineers to identify and mitigate biases present in the system – underscoring a need for more explainable AI technologies that allow us greater insight into how decisions made by machines were arrived at.

Fairness Definitions and Trade-Offs: Establishing what qualifies as fair behavior from an algorithmic perspective isn't easy as different fairness metrics often conflict with each other - requiring careful consideration not just around equitable decision-making but also accuracy and efficiency requirements too.

Accountability and Responsibility: It's important not to lose sight of who ultimately has responsibility for ensuring the ethical use of technology. Appropriate measures should be put in place to clearly define roles and responsibilities across all stakeholders involved, including providers, users, regulators, etc.

Unlocking Passive Income with ChatGPT

Taking these issues seriously can create responsible Artificial Intelligence solutions that benefit society rather than harm it.

The Road to Ethical and Inclusive AI: Taking Action

Data Diversity and Representation: Ensuring a diverse range of data is essential to avoiding biased AI systems. Achieving inclusivity should be the priority when collecting info - plus, pre-processing needs to be done properly.

Fairness Techniques: To prioritize fairness, researchers have come up with algorithms like fairness mindful learning algos, bias controlling tactics and, impartiality constraints while training models.

Transparency and Explainability: Enhancing transparency and explainability makes it simpler to detect existing biases within Artificial Intelligence programs. Interpretable machine-learning techniques and model-agnostic explanations allow for better decisions made by AI.

Collaborative Efforts and Policy Crafting: Tackling bias in AI demands collaboration between experts, policymakers, and advocacy groups alike - having conversations and creating laws that promote accountability are key here.

Ensuring Explainability and Transparency in AI Algorithms

As data is increasingly being shared online, safeguarding privacy is more important than ever. But with Artificial Intelligence becoming more sophisticated and able to detect subtle patterns that humans may miss, individuals are at risk of having their personal information used without even realizing it. This raises serious concerns about violations of rights and freedoms. That leads to considering both positive aspects of advances in AI technology as well as potential dangers like unauthorized access to private data a must.

The Potential for Violation of Privacy Rights and Freedoms

In this digital era, safeguarding privacy rights is of paramount importance, especially when it comes to AI-powered tech tools like ChatGPT. We need to harness all available resources, which range from encryption methods and biometric authentication to stringent regulatory policies that monitor how businesses and organizations handle sensitive user data. Raising awareness about responsible data management practices is also crucial in ensuring the security of present and future generations utilizing these AI-driven tools.

ChatGPT, being a sophisticated AI language model, can potentially have access to a wealth of personal information. This highlights the necessity for robust measures to prevent any misuse of such sensitive data. If not appropriately protected, unscrupulous entities could exploit this information for harmful activities, including identity theft or cyberbullying, emphasizing the importance of rigorous safeguards around personal data handled by AI tools like ChatGPT.

The Consequences of AI Bias and Discrimination

AI technology has the potential to be incredibly powerful—but it also carries a unique risk. Our AI algorithms must be regularly monitored for bias and trained with diverse datasets. Any existing bias in the data used will directly affect outcomes, which could result in unfair decisions based on factors such as race, gender, or economic status. By taking these proactive steps, one can shape an equitable future and protect against discrimination of any kind.

While privacy might not seem related at first glance, there's actually an intimate connection between the two issues of bias in AI and personal information protection. The reason for this lies in how many current AI technologies use data collected from online activities, social media posts, or public records in order to make decisions – which often reveals elements about a person's life like their religious beliefs or political views (among others).

When these systems contain biases against certain groups of people – whether conscious or unconscious – it ultimately leads to adverse outcomes that harm individuals directly and perpetuate systemic injustices within society.

Take hiring practices as an example: if an employer uses discriminatory AIs during their job application process, those belonging to certain backgrounds may be unfairly excluded solely because of their identity rather than any real qualifications they possess. That would take away potential opportunities that could have otherwise helped them break out into new career paths - resulting in nothing short of a modern-day glass ceiling for some minority communities everywhere.

AI and Privacy: Toeing the Line of Balance

In this digital age, Artificial Intelligence (AI) has become a game-changer in multiple aspects of life. From generative AI that can create any content with a simple prompt to smart home devices that learn your habits and preferences, AI's potential is remarkable. With data growing exponentially over time, though, questions surrounding privacy have also been on the rise. As the exploration of this topic continues, it's important to consider how exactly AI affects users' personal information and privacy rights.

Real-World Instances of AI-Related Privacy Issues

CASE 1: Google Location Tracking Controversy

Google came under fire back in 2018 when an Associated Press investigation revealed they were tracking user locations even when said users did not give permission. This caused immense backlash from consumers and advocates who protested against Google's lack of trustworthiness towards its customers' private details – leading them to change their policies regarding location tracking since then. However, despite these modifications, doubts about how data is collected, used, or accessed remain. Leading to the realization of just how much power one tech giant holds over individuals' security online today.

One of the biggest worries with Google's tracking practices is how personal data can be misused. Location information carries huge risks if it falls into the wrong hands and could result in dire consequences like surveillance or criminal activity.

To keep privacy concerns in mind, companies need to ensure their security protocols are up-to-date. But third parties access to user information adds another layer of danger - advertisers cash in on this information while other organizations might buy it for financial gain.

CASE 2. AI-Powered Recommendations: My Experience with Google's Suggestion Engine

As the world of Artificial Intelligence rapidly develops, privacy is becoming an increasing concern. Just recently, I was reminded of this in my own life. After streaming a show on Amazon Prime through Apple TV, two days later, Google's app on my iPhone had suggestions related to it - even though I didn't even watch it there! That highlights just how much tech giants know about their users.

Having worked with large amounts of information for years now, I'm aware that AI makes these kinds of insights possible - but they're still unsettling if not properly regulated. Google's recommendation algorithm brings up another important point; how crucial are privacy measures in a time where AI advancements are happening so quickly? And what happens when personalized advice appears without any input from other devices or conversations being monitored by microphones? This issue needs real attention before Big Tech gains too much access to our lives without us knowing about it.

These tactics should not be allowed as they violate basic human rights and values when it comes to protecting personal information. To ensure such practices aren't taking place unchecked going forward, companies need to take steps now to create stricter guidelines regarding the use of AI, while policymakers must also create regulations designed to protect individuals' right to keep their data private at all times.

The Cultural and Social Impact of ChatGPT

ChatGPT is a prime example of the transformative potential of AI in reshaping how people create and consume content. It has democratized access to a wide audience, allowing more people to engage with AI than ever before. Yet, this progress is not without its pitfalls. We must be aware of challenges such as automated deception, uneven information distribution, and potential data breaches that come with the territory of AI deployment in cultural and social spheres.

ChatGPT is fundamentally altering human communication. By substituting traditional face-to-face conversations with machine-mediated dialogues, it introduces a new dynamic that can strain interpersonal relationships. Machines equipped with emotion-detecting technologies may inadvertently misinterpret or overlook subtleties that are intrinsic to human communication. Thus, it's crucial to consider the implications of these advancements on daily life and strive for an environment where intelligent systems do not perpetuate discrimination or exploitation.

On the other hand, the integration of AI like ChatGPT into various use-cases presents numerous advantages. Improved customer service via responsive chatbots and accurate data analysis are just the tip of the iceberg. However, regardless of future advancements, it is imperative to institute measures that protect privacy and ensure the impartiality of algorithm decisions.

ChatGPT-driven chatbots are becoming a popular, cost-effective solution for large-scale customer service operations. Despite their convenience and speed, these chatbots cannot fully replicate the human connection that emerges from real conversations with customers. Their potential failure to accurately interpret emotional cues from users can lead to subpar experiences. This highlights the irreplaceable value of human involvement in areas where technology currently falls short.

The story of ChatGPT is a testament to the ways in which AI has revolutionized culture in recent years. However, it is also a cautionary tale that reminds us of the risks associated with AI-powered products and services. We must not overlook the need for robust methods of detecting bias in AI systems, as well as safeguards for privacy and civil rights, prior to deploying any new AI-powered system.

AI and Cybersecurity: Safeguarding Data and Networks

The potential of AI on businesses, customers, and cybercriminals is a double-edged sword. Voice recognition technology like Alexa has become an integral part of everyday life. Search engines such as Google have revolutionized the way people access information.

Moreover, certain financial organizations are using AI to prevent fraudulent activities, saving them billions yearly. Yet the utilization of AI in cyber security raises questions about its potential for enhancing or weakening digital security for companies.

What Challenges Does Cyber Security Face?

Cyber security faces many challenges, including:

- A vast attack surface area.

- An extensive number of devices need protection within an organization.

- Numerous attack vectors are used by hackers.

- A lack of skilled security professionals due to ever-growing demands.

- Too much data with too little human capacity needed to process it all accurately – making analysis increasingly difficult

What Is the Reach of AI in Cyber Security?

In the realm of cyber safety, artificial intelligence, specifically ChatGPT, presents both opportunities and challenges. While it enhances our ability to analyze, understand, and thwart malicious activities to protect user information and business assets, it also presents an avenue for wrongdoers to leverage this technology for nefarious purposes. A notable application of AI in this context is virtual private networks (VPNs). Machine learning gives them an upper hand in mitigating online threats that stem from AI itself!

As we advance further into the digital age, anticipating and neutralizing cyber threats is crucial. With AI-infused security solutions like ChatGPT at our disposal, we stand a better chance against online adversaries. The sophisticated algorithms of machine learning and AI offer a competitive edge, swiftly processing data and providing robust defense mechanisms. The time to capitalize on these advanced technologies is now! View them as shields, defending us from potential digital hazards.

The 10 Benefits of Using AI in Cybersecurity

Seeking success in the digital age? AI can get you there. With over 200,000 cyber events aiming to take down mid-sized companies each day, it's critical that businesses deploy advanced technology for maximum protection of their networks and data. Artificial intelligence is a powerful tool for combatting threats, recognizing new malware types, and safeguarding sensitive info—all key ingredients when it comes to staying safe online.

Instead of relying on human experts who struggle to manually address every alert (an impossible task due to the huge volume of attacks), AI systems are able to process vast amounts of info faster and more accurately, preventing any breach from slipping through the cracks! If your business wants to stay ahead in today's ever-evolving tech world, then AI is an essential component for keeping secure. Here're ten ways this cutting-edge intel can boost cybersecurity:

1. Get Smarter Over Time

AI has the ability to analyze network activity as they occur - detecting anomalies or incidents that don't line up with normal behavior patterns right away so hackers have no chance of outsmarting it.

2. Unknown Threats Identified Instantly

Keeping tabs on unknown threats used to be tough, but now Artificial Intelligence automates this process by quickly scanning through data sets - allowing you to detect potential danger before it does damage.

3. Handle Data Easily

With vast amounts of traffic flowing through company networks on a daily basis, manually reviewing all activity isn't feasible; however, AI technology automatically scans and identifies disguised threats so businesses can focus their attention elsewhere without compromising safety measures.

4. Vulnerability Management

Cybersecurity personnel often have difficulty pinpointing weak points within existing systems when faced with numerous targets – luckily though, Artificial Intelligence is well-equipped to handle such tasks due to its self-learning capabilities! This helps businesses fix problems quicker while also preventing attacks from occurring beforehand too.

5. Overall Security Boosted

Human error is inevitable; mistakes happen every day, which makes solidifying overall security measures even harder. Fortunately, using automated processes powered by Artificial

Intelligence means you won't miss anything important. This eliminates risk and allows companies to prioritize prevention against multiple looming dangers simultaneously, giving them one less thing worth worrying about, no matter how sophisticated the tactics get over time.

6. Streamlining Security Systems

AI has completely transformed the game when it comes to cyber security, automating tiresome and repetitive tasks that could otherwise lead to human error or complacency. It's like having an extra pair of eyes on watch - all day, every day - scanning large amounts of data for potential threats and ensuring businesses stay up-to-date with their network safety protocols at all times.

7. Rapidly Detecting and Responding

Integrating AI into digital defense is a total game changer in terms of detection speed. With it malicious activity can be spotted faster than ever before, allowing for immediate action before any irreversible damage is done. This frees up humans from tedious manual scans so they can focus more intently on higher-level strategies instead.

8. Strengthening Authentication Processes

Websites featuring user accounts or contact forms with sensitive info require an added layer of protection - one that AI is uniquely suited for providing, thanks to its ability to recognize patterns better than traditional methods like CAPTCHAs or fingerprint scanners. It can handle even complex authentication scenarios efficiently while protecting against credential stuffing attacks and brute force attempts leading up to a possible breach in your network's defenses.

9. Reducing Manual Labor

With AI reducing the amount of tedious labor needed, human experts no longer have to waste countless hours performing mundane scans but rather use them as opportunities to hone their skillset and further refine strategies combatting emerging cyber threats more effectively.

10. Battling Bots

To protect against bots used maliciously spreading malware and stealing data, Artificial Intelligence provides invaluable assistance by recognizing patterns within bot behavior. It deploys honeypots, capturing and blocking them effectively and learning how to adapt new tactics for bypassing existing safeguards.

AI and Employment: Upskilling and Reskilling the Workforce

The AI revolution has made experts with specialized skills a must for the ever-changing landscape of today. According to LinkedIn's 2020 report, demand for tech wizards is soaring due to companies favoring automation over manual labor. Although this advancement can make our lives simpler by taking on mundane tasks, it also brings forth certain risks like job insecurity and widening the already huge divide between those who have access to education and those who don't.

This is why upskilling and reskilling are nowadays seen as go-to solutions businesses use to stay ahead of revolutionary technology changes. Upskilling allows organizations to develop their existing employees' abilities through extra training, while reskilling gives them whole new areas of knowledge - preparing them for positions they may be unaware exist! So if you want your business to keep up and dominate in this fast-paced world, equip yourself or your team with these valuable skills now.

The Power of Reskilling and Upskilling

As AI continues to revolutionize the job market, upskilling and reskilling are invaluable tools when it comes to keeping your team ahead of the curve. By acquiring new skills or refreshing old ones, workers can easily adjust their abilities in order to keep pace with technological advancements – allowing them to remain just as competitive no matter how quickly things change. Here are a few key areas that companies should consider investing in:

Data Analysis: With AI becoming increasingly integral to businesses worldwide, data analytics is an essential skill for professionals across all industries - from salespeople needing sophisticated CRM systems which use AI algorithms for customer predictions based on past buying activities right through IT experts and software developers who require proficiency working around ML technologies.

AI and Machine Learning Knowledge: As tech evolves evermore rapidly into more complex territories, everyone needs a basic understanding of Artificial Intelligence (AI) and machine learning (ML). Not only does this ensure you stay relevant moving forward, but it also gives you an edge over competitors still stuck in outdated methods - so if you want success tomorrow, then don't sleep on these must-have techniques.

Digital Literacy and Cybersecurity Skills: As society moves towards a future where Artificial Intelligence plays a bigger role than ever before, having digital literacy is now essential for any employee looking to stay ahead in the game - whether they're creating content or using online tools powered by AI. To ensure that all businesses reap maximum benefits from their investments in such technologies without running afoul of security policies at the same time, reskilling employees in cybersecurity should also be a high priority when upskilling staff members across different departments within an organization.

Boosting Employee Morale and Retention

Keeping employee morale and loyalty high doesn't have to be complicated. Invest in your team's growth by giving them opportunities for upskilling or reskilling. They'll know you value their development, resulting in greater commitment and satisfaction. Plus, it's a solution where everyone benefits. Yes, everyone benefits from the investment.

Examples:

Career Advancement Possibilities: Employers that offer upskilling opportunities make clear to their staff there's a chance for professional growth within the organization. A customer service rep, for instance? They can get trained in superior communication tactics and leadership abilities. As such, their current job performance can be improved while giving them a path toward personal development - resulting in contentedness and loyalty to the company.

Individual Development Programs: Reinvigorate your team with reskilling. Introduce coding classes to employees in non-technical departments - it's a great way for them to learn something new and explore potential job opportunities. Investing in personnel development shows you care, plus it'll give everyone an extra morale boost too. **Adaptability during Changes**: Adapt or get left behind. Reskilling courses are perfect for industries where technology is rapidly evolving, like manufacturing; workers won't have to worry about their roles becoming redundant as automation takes over if they're upskilled in robot maintenance or programming. Education businesses should show their commitment by providing these programs – not only now but also looking ahead into the future. With creative minds from different disciplines working together, the possibilities are endless, and more efficient solutions can be implemented immediately.

Cross-Functional Collaboration: Stepping outside of the comfort zone and upskilling or reskilling employees in areas beyond their primary role can bring a fresh, creative outlook to any project. For instance, say you've got an ace marketer who has recently been trained in data analysis; when this person partners with your data science team, they have the potential to craft strategies that blend both artistry and analytics for maximum impact.

Efficiency in Problem-Solving: With diverse skillsets, problem-solving becomes faster and more efficient. Take for instance a project manager who is familiar with coding; this allows them to better understand software development issues while allowing them to communicate quickly with developers for quicker resolution of said issues which ultimately streamlines the project's execution process.

Innovation in Product Development: Upskilling or reskilling also leads to much-needed innovation when it comes to product design and buildout - think aesthetically pleasing user experiences (UX) from those who have been upskilled. This means products created now meet customer needs easier as well as stand out amongst the competition - all thanks to an understanding of UX principles.

AI and Human Decision-Making: Striking the Perfect Balance

As tech capabilities continue to grow, Artificial Intelligence is becoming increasingly useful in structured environments with clearly defined goals and limited inputs/outputs. Take a parts distribution machine at a manufacturing plant for example – AI armed with real-time feedback of usage on the factory floor and urgent requests can process information quickly and accurately, delivering whatever parts are needed exactly when they're necessary for just-in-time engineering. This leads to fewer accidents, injuries, or delays due to human error. Plus, it's way faster than any person could manage alone.

So can you ensure AI systems strike the perfect balance between automation and human input? Assuming all variables remain controlled while still allowing variation in certain circumstances, an algorithm must be implemented which takes into account every possible input and output and then processes them accordingly to maximize benefits while solving complex problems efficiently. In other words: let machines handle what they're good at but don't forget about us humans either – because, sometimes, there's no substitute for our unique logic!

Humans have the gift of ingenuity, but it takes time to make complex decisions. In today's world, where businesses need to consider an immense number of factors when looking at potential acquisitions or partnerships, AI can be used as a tool to help human minds navigate these challenging choices quickly and efficiently.

Instead of spending days analyzing data points by hand, Artificial Intelligence (AI) can be employed for comprehensive processing capabilities that provide a clear overview. That way, it allows for more energy and resources to weigh the pros and cons before making a final decision on any given issue.

Take buying out another company, for example. There are so many components involved like design history, market conditions, current staff productivity levels, payroll absorption implications, etc. All of them need careful consideration in order to form an informed conclusion about whether or not it's worth taking this step forward into uncharted waters – something humans haven't been able to maximize alone until now.

The power of AI-aided Intelligence Amplification is perhaps best seen in situations requiring such nuanced judgment calls, where technology helps speed up the process without sacrificing detail quality. It frees up the human cognition space needed for strategic planning and creative problem solving – some things just require those special touches only we humans possess!

As an entrepreneur, I'm in the pursuit of my dreams, and AI is part of that journey. Although it has come far, there's still much work to be done before it can replace me in running a business effectively – something which requires expertise from all angles: staff, family, friends, and mentors all give valuable input, which contributes to an individual knowledge bank that allows sound decision making for multiple facets within the startup world.

However, AI does help me when considering complex scenarios. For instance, analytics tools help determine my next move by providing insight into website performance. Plus, they make me more efficient. People may not even realize they're using Artificial Intelligence every day, but its presence is definitely felt - so embrace this technological revolution.

The Role of Regulations and Policies in ChatGPT

Regulations and policies play a crucial role in the development, use, and management of AI technologies like ChatGPT. These rules and guidelines are set in place to ensure the ethical, responsible, and safe use of AI, and to prevent misuse or abuse.

Here are some of the areas where regulations and policies come into play:

1. **Data Protection and Privacy**: ChatGPT and similar models are trained on large amounts of data, which may include personal or sensitive information. Policies and regulations like GDPR in the European Union, and other data protection laws

worldwide, guide how this data should be handled to protect individuals' privacy.

2. **Fairness and Bias**: AI models can unintentionally perpetuate or amplify biases present in the training data. Regulations and policies can ensure that these technologies are developed and used in a way that minimizes these biases and promotes fairness.

3. **Transparency and Explainability**: AI decisions can sometimes be hard to understand due to their complex and opaque decision-making processes. Regulations can enforce transparency and explainability in AI operations, helping users understand how decisions are made.

4. **Misuse of Technology**: There are concerns about the potential misuse of AI technology, such as spreading disinformation, creating deepfakes, or performing automated attacks. Policies can help prevent and penalize such misuse.

5. **Accountability and Responsibility**: When errors or harmful outcomes occur, it's important to have policies in place that assign responsibility and accountability.

6. **Intellectual Property**: AI technologies can generate content that could infringe on existing copyrights or create new content that may require protection. Policies help define who owns AI-generated content and how intellectual property rights apply.

OpenAI has a set of principles and guidelines to ensure the responsible and ethical use of its technologies, and complies with existing regulations. As AI technology continues to advance, it's important that regulations and policies evolve alongside it to address new challenges and concerns.

Chapter 7: Building Your AI Skills and Expertise

This chapter serves as a guide to help you learn and acquire practical knowledge that will enable you to excel in the field of AI. Whether you are a beginner or have some prior experience, this book is here to support your learning journey as you develop the necessary skills to navigate the dynamic landscape of artificial intelligence.

Learning AI: Courses, Resources, and Certifications

With Artificial Intelligence (AI) on the rise, now's the time to gear up for a career in this field. According to IDC's projections, revenues from AI software are expected to skyrocket and reach $596 billion by 2025 - that's an impressive 17.7% CAGR! To help you get ahead of the curve and stay competitive in this rapidly evolving industry, getting certified in AI technologies is important. Investing your energy into learning about these tools can open doors for exciting opportunities and make employers view you as an expert in AI-related solutions.

Stanford University School of Engineering AI Graduate Program

Key Elements:

The Stanford University School of Engineering is offering a highly sought-after Artificial Intelligence Graduate Program. Dive into the fundamentals and technologies at the core of AI, such as logic, probability models, machine learning algorithms, robotics systems, natural language processing capabilities, and knowledge representation methods. Discover how machines can be used to solve problems or interact with one another through reasoning and learning processes - then design your own tests for implementation!

To successfully complete this program, you'll need to earn a 3.0 GPA or higher in each course which consists of 1 required class plus three electives tailored to your interests.

Requirements for Admission:

If you want to jump into the deep end of higher education, here's what you'll need. First and foremost, a bachelor's degree with an impressive 3.0 GPA or above is essential; furthermore, having mastery over prerequisites like stats and probability, linear algebra, and calculus is key! Plus, don't forget your programming chops - think C/C++, Java, or Python (or something similar). Note that each course could have its own set of additional prerequisites, so make sure to check them off too.

1. **Designing and Building Artificial Intelligence Products and Services by MIT xPro**

Key Elements:

Take your understanding of AI to the next level with this 8-week certificate program. Dive into the four stages of creating an AI-based product, from concept to completion. Explore machine and deep learning algorithms that will help you solve real-world challenges. Plus, put your newfound knowledge into practice as you craft a proposal for stakeholders and investors – it's ShowTime! Get ready to become an AI expert.

Requirements for Admission:

UX/UI designers, tech professionals, consultants, entrepreneurs, technical product managers, and AI startup founders

2. **AI: Business Strategies and Applications by UC Berkeley Executive Education and Emeritus**

Key Elements:

This certificate program is designed for managers who are leading AI teams — not teaching the technical aspects of AI development. It will introduce you to essential applications of Artificial Intelligence in business and discuss its current capabilities, uses, potential risks, and opportunities.

You'll also get a comprehensive overview of automation, machine learning, deep learning, neural networks, computer vision, and robotics. Discover how to build an effective AI team from scratch as well as manage successful projects involving AI applications. Plus, gain insights into technology-related topics so you can communicate clearly with your tech squad and co-workers.

Prerequisites:

Ideal candidates include C-suite executives and senior managers, data scientists, analysts, and mid-career professionals looking to advance their skillset in Artificial Intelligence technologies — all ready to embark upon this fascinating journey together.

3. IBM Applied AI Professional Certificate (via Coursera)

Key Elements:

Ready to get your Artificial Intelligence expertise started? This beginner-level AI certification course is here to help bring you up to speed. You'll understand what's at the core of artificial intelligence, its applications and use cases, and machine learning concepts like deep learning and neural networks - no problem! Using IBM Watson

AI services, APIs, and Python (with minimal coding skills necessary!), it will equip you with the tools needed to create virtual assistants and chatbots that can be deployed onto websites without any programming knowledge. Lastly, this course will also teach computer vision techniques using OpenCV and Watson so you can develop custom image classification models and deploy them in the cloud.

Prerequisites:

It doesn't matter if your background is technical, everyone's invited! Just note that an introductory Python course is included for those without a programming background before diving into building/deploying those sweet AI apps.

4. Artificial Intelligence for Everyone by Andrew Ng (via Coursera)

Key Elements:

This course is a nontechnical exploration of AI, looking into the definitions and implications of common terms like neural networks, machine learning, deep learning, and data science. You'll learn what AI can -and cannot- do for you or your company, how to spot potential opportunities to apply it, the feeling of building ML projects from scratch, working with AI teams efficiently, and formulating effective strategies in organizations.

Plus, getting those tough conversations about ethics out there!

Prerequisites:

Open to everyone regardless of background knowledge.

5. Introduction to TensorFlow for AI, Deep Learning, and Machine Learning (via Coursera)

Key Elements:

Are you a software developer aspiring to become an AI-powered algorithm expert? Then this Deep Learning and AI TensorFlow Developer Professional Certificate program is just what you need! It covers the best practices for using TensorFlow, an open-source machine learning framework - teaching students how to create basic neural networks and use convolutions to improve them.

Prerequisites:

There's no prior knowledge of machine or deep learning required. All that's needed is high school-level math and experience with Python coding.

Developing Programming Skills for AI

AI programming skills are the capabilities necessary to thrive as an AI programmer in a field that utilizes artificial intelligence. Key objectives of utilizing an AI-based program or algorithm include:

- Replacing people on recurrent and relatively simple duties

- Outperforming the human brain when it comes to learning and memorizing

- Instantly recognizing patterns and making decisions based on them

To master Artificial Intelligence, here's what you should do:

1. Get your High School Diploma

To become involved in Artificial Intelligence engineering, getting a high school diploma with a specialization in scientific disciplines like mathematics, physics or chemistry is essential. You can also add statistics to your educational background for more success later on. Having these solid foundations through secondary education will give you major advantages going forward.

2. Earn Your Bachelor's Degree

If you're looking for ways to stand out from other applicants while pursuing careers related to AI engineering, consider enrolling in either a three-year B.Sc. (Bachelor of Science) program or a four-year B.Tech. (Bachelor of Technology) degree course specializing specifically within this area alongside data science and machine learning studies, too, if desired. However, if NITs, IITs, and IIITs are where you wish to study, make sure to ace the Joint Entrance Examination (JEE) first.

3. Get Your Master's Degree

Further boosting job opportunities and earning potential by acquiring yourself an MSc focusing solely on Artificial Intelligence would prove highly beneficial, too, so don't forget about this option as well, given its many benefits over time.

4. Earn Professional Credentials

Gaining proficiency in AI and ML doesn't have to break the bank. You can become an ace engineer without spending all your hard-earned cash. Consider taking part in diploma programs or postgraduate courses for a structured learning experience.

With guidance from experienced professionals, you'll be able to work on real-world projects with feedback along the way. By combining theoretical knowledge with practical experience, you're sure to join the ever-growing field of AI.

5. Grow Your Expertise through Experience

To reach peak performance as an AI expert, it's essential that you get hands-on practice with actual problems out there. Through participating in hackathons and completing projects, you can hone your capabilities using different toolsets used by industry experts – plus earn yourself some major street cred! And if classroom instruction isn't quite for you - don't worry; online tutorials are just as effective at teaching these cutting-edge technologies.

6. Reap the Rewards of Your Hard Work

Finally, what kind of compensation could one expect after all the hard work? According to Glassdoor statistics, being an AI engineer pays off both here in America (with an average annual salary of $114k) or overseas ($765k annually). Although salaries may vary depending on organization size and individual skillset - rest assured that investing time into honing your craft will reap big rewards down the road.

Exploring AI Frameworks and Libraries

AI development is made simpler by Python's extensive libraries and frameworks. With pre-built functions and tools, developers can save time creating AI systems. Below are some of the top Python libraries used in Artificial Intelligence.

TensorFlow is the ultimate go-to for developing advanced AI applications. As Google's premier deep learning library, it's become a favorite among developers - both amateur and pro. With its intuitive design, you can quickly construct powerful neural networks that train on gargantuan datasets. Plus, TensorFlow supports all kinds of platforms from Android to iOS and the web - ensuring your cutting-edge AI apps are available anywhere! To top things off with a contemporary flair, references to modern pop culture abound throughout TensorFlow, so creating Artificial Intelligence has never been simpler or more fun.

With the rise of artificial intelligence, two frameworks have come to dominate the space: Keras and Scikit-Learn. For those just getting their feet wet in deep learning, Keras is a great place to start thanks to its simple yet powerful user interface - it's easy enough for any novice developer to use but still supports complex experimentation with neural networks. With an active community always ready with support when you need it, this high-level API is quickly becoming beloved by AI enthusiasts around the world!

But if you're looking for something more advanced that offers serious results fast, look no further than Scikit-learn. This Python library gives users access to all sorts of supervised and unsupervised algorithms designed specifically for classification and clustering purposes - plus everything else needed to create quality models swiftly and efficiently. And unlike other libraries out there whose documentation can be confusingly technical or overcomplicated at times, this one explains things so clearly even rookies will know exactly what they're doing each step of the way.

PyTorch, the brainchild of Facebook's AI Research team, is a powerful open-source toolkit for Artificial Intelligence development. It stands out in deep learning and provides an adaptable platform to easily create and train neural networks. One of its chief advantages is its dynamic computation graph which allows developers to modify the network architecture during runtime - enabling faster experimentation! Plus, PyTorch offers flexibility when it comes to testing models quickly and iterating as needed.

NLTK (Natural Language Toolkit) has become an essential Python library for working with human language data. This invaluable resource covers everything from tokenization and stemming all the way up to part-of-speech tagging - making it perfect for those creating NLP projects such as chatbots or virtual assistants. NLTK's wide array of features makes it ideal for tackling complex tasks within this space while offering plenty of room for customization.

Hands-on AI Projects

In an ever-evolving world of Artificial Intelligence, tech fanatics have a plethora of opportunities to explore and create groundbreaking projects. From the research that pushes the boundaries of what's possible to everyday applications, AI is making huge strides in our lives – it can be seen everywhere, from Spotify playlist curation to Instagram feeds.

As AI continues its rapid growth over the next few years, companies like IBM, Accenture, and Apple predict that by 2025 this industry will be worth $126 Billion US Dollars!

So where do you start? Well, there are plenty of options out there.

Lane Line Detection

Aim: To develop an AI-driven system that can accurately detect lane lines on roads in real-time, assisting self-driving cars and line-following robots alike.

Problem: Autonomous vehicles have the potential to revolutionize transportation, but careless programming could lead to disastrous incidents - a risk we must mitigate. As such, it is vital for these vehicles to be able to recognize lane lines while they are driving so as not to put anyone else at risk.

Solution: Computer Vision techniques implemented with OpenCV are perfect for this task due to their ability to access all major platforms (Windows, macOS, Linux, Android, and iOS) and quickly process data in order for autonomous cars or robots to make judgments about their surroundings without any human input.

By using CV tactics such as color thresholding or frame masking on NumPy arrays, you can easily find white markers along each side of lanes that serve as navigational signals while driving down roads. Applying Hough line transformations will then help pinpoint these lane lines more precisely, ensuring they're visible during navigation providing your autonomous car with an extra layer of security like Tony Stark's AI assistant Jarvis!

Application: Lane line detection is an essential tool for modern-day autonomous vehicles, from cars to robots that follow a predetermined path. It's also widely used in the gaming industry - think of all those high-octane racing games on PlayStation and Xbox! With lane line detection, developers can create an ultra-realistic driving experience that puts players firmly in the driver's seat with total control over their virtual ride. This tech is also immensely useful for testing out innovative self-driving technology before introducing it to reality on streets and highways.

Plus, you get a chance to relive your favorite movie car chase scenes without leaving your couch.

Chatbots

Aim: Bring your web or app platform to the next level with a Python-powered chatbot that provides users with an awesome experience.

Problem: In this digital age, it's more important than ever for companies to keep their customers engaged and satisfied. Failing to do so can be detrimental, resulting in lost revenue and missed opportunities.

Solution: Chatbots are essential if you want to stay ahead of the competition! Powered by AI, these bots provide 24/7 automated customer service - from answering questions and navigating through websites or apps to personalizing experiences and boosting sales. Plus, they offer incredible insights into user behavior, allowing businesses to tweak products and services for optimum success. It's time to give your platforms a facelift - get yourself a chatbot now.

If it's time to get on board with building your own chatbot, then have no fear; taking those first steps is relatively straightforward. Begin by researching which structure works best for other websites and doing something similar before moving on to applying Natural Language Processing (NLP) technology. These are algorithms that understand human interactions across multiple languages plus audio signals, text analysis, and conversion into machine language. Once all these elements come together, it'll be like having an intelligent assistant ready at hand 24/7!

Applications: Chatbots are now being used by everyone from eCommerce giants like Amazon Alexa and Spotify to real estate firms such as Marriott International and Pizza Hut; Customer Service departments alongside IT Helpdesk teams in Sales Marketing and HR alike rely heavily on them every day. Don't miss out - make sure your business has one today if it doesn't already.

Voice-Based Virtual Assistant

Aim: Crafting a revolutionary app that makes life easier.

Problem: With the vastness of the Internet, it can be hard to locate exactly what you need. Not to mention we are always on the go and don't have time for mundane tasks.

Solution: Enter virtual assistants with their remarkable Natural Language Processing (NLP) capabilities, such as Alexa or Siri - they understand your needs before you even voice them out. They save your queries in databases, so when you ask for something again, they already know about it. Plus, these apps easily convert words into text and vice versa - just like magic.

Application: Finding things quickly is only one aspect of the abilities of virtual assistants. But there's more; from playing music to showing movies or sending reminders – whatever task you need to be done will be handled by your trusty assistant with finesse. So go ahead and take advantage of all modern technology has to offer– just ask away without hesitation because no matter how crazy life gets, help is here waiting for you.

Plagiarism Checker

Aim: Develop an AI-powered system to effectively identify and detect plagiarism in any document.

Problem: Plagiarists are doing serious damage - from tarnishing reputations to flagrantly disregarding copyright laws and putting people at risk of legal repercussions. Organizations need a reliable solution that can help them combat this growing problem.

Solution: By combining Python Flask with text mining technology, you can create the ultimate anti-plagiarism tool. It is not your average checker, either. Bolstered by the Pinecone vector database, it will be able to quickly spot copied material in documents with ease!

Application: Goodbye plagiarizers - hello originality! Bloggers, editors/publishers evaluating manuscripts, or freelancers creating content for clients.

Games

Aim: Craft Epic Video Games with AI.

Problem: Gamers are always looking for more realistic, immersive digital experiences.

Solution: Step up your game and supercharge the realism in video games with Artificial Intelligence. Think of cool stuff like chatbots, voice recognition, Natural Language Processing (NLP), image processing tools, and data mining algorithms combined with some next-level machine learning techniques.

Application: Be prepared to be amazed by incredible AI-powered video games such as AlphaGo from Google DeepMind, the all-time chess champion Deep Blue from IBM, the FEAR series brought to you by Monolith Productions, and Microsoft Studios' legendary Halo franchise. By merging your project ideas with advanced AI capabilities, you will become a programming pro and get involved in amazing tech like NLP and Data Science - making every gamer jump out of their seat in excitement.

Building a Career in AI

Welcome to the thrilling world of AI and ML, where opportunities are boundless, and rewards abound. Strap in because this realm is about to take off like a rocket ship - you won't want to miss out on this wild ride. Just ask Ray Kurzweil, who insists that by 2029 machines will have achieved human-level intelligence.

But wait! There is more. He also predicts that our civilization's machine smartness could be multiplied up to one billion times by 2045 - it's as if Artificial Intelligence is the wish-granting genie from Aladdin! So, if you're ready for an adventure of a lifetime and make your mark on history, then look no further – seize this golden opportunity now before it slips away.

Here are five game-changing roles in the AI and ML universe:

1. Machine Learning Engineer

ML engineers are responsible for programming machines to do specific tasks while also managing and constructing machine learning platforms. If you have an academic background in programming or engineering, this role would be perfect for you since it will help with an easy transition into other similar roles too.

It is necessary that ML engineers possess knowledge of various coding languages such as Python, Java, and Scala; they should also know how to handle large datasets using utilities like R and SQL efficiently whilst applying predictive models on them correctly, following big data best practices.

Alongside this, experience with agile development techniques and leading tools (like IntelliJ/Eclipse) is desirable when looking into becoming an engineer. Plus, if you can add the cherry on top by having either a Master's degree or a Doctoral degree related to computer science or mathematics, then your CV will stand out from the rest.

2. Data Scientist

If you want to be the Tony Stark of your organization and turn heads with your tech game, then here's what it takes: A master's or doctoral degree in computer science is a must-have for any aspiring data scientist.

But don't sweat if that's not in the books just yet - expertise with cloud tools like Hadoop or Amazon S3 along with two years' worth of machine learning experience, can still take you places.

Data scientists are our modern-day wizards who work their magic on massive datasets using predictive analytics and ML techniques. They create pipelines powered by Spark, MapReduce, Hive, and Pig; coding languages such as SQL, Python, Perl, and Scala; and models that make sense of this information, all while keeping up with today's ever-changing technology landscape. These experts help organizations make fast and informed decisions like never before.

3. Business Intelligence (BI) Developer

Are you ready to dive into an awesome journey as a business intelligence programmer? In today's complicated market, these master coders hold the key to success. They dig deep into intricate datasets, uncover concealed patterns and understand what keeps the industry running. To make data more accessible and tractable, they work their secret powers of analytics on cloud platforms.

To thrive in this epic job role, there are certain skills required: top-notch analysis acumen plus technical know-how; problem-solving chops with great communication abilities (to liaise with those who don't speak tech), along with having a bachelor's degree in computer science or related field - bonus points if you can wield SQL queries and data mining/warehouse designs and BI technologies. Experience is not compulsory but certainly welcomed!

4. Research Scientist

Research scientists in artificial intelligence (AI) work to advance the theoretical understanding of AI concepts and create new AI technologies and applications. Their work involves conducting research, designing and running experiments, publishing papers, and presenting findings at conferences.

Some of the main areas of research in AI include:

1. Machine learning: Developing algorithms that allow computers to improve automatically through experience. This includes areas like deep learning, reinforcement learning, etc.

2. Natural language processing: Research focused on giving computers the ability to understand and manipulate human language.

3. Computer vision: Using AI to help computers "see" and interpret visual images and video.

4. Robotics: Developing intelligent autonomous robots through the use of AI and machine learning.

To become a research scientist in AI, you will typically need:

1. An advanced degree, often a Ph.D., in a relevant field like computer science, electrical engineering, cognitive science, or math. A master's in computer science can also work for some positions.

2. Strong programming skills in languages like Python, R, and Java. Knowledge of frameworks like TensorFlow and PyTorch is often required.

3. Excellent problem-solving abilities and the capability to conduct independent research and experiments.

4. The ability to clearly communicate and publish findings through research papers and conference presentations.

5. Curiosity, creativity, and an interest in pushing the boundaries of what's possible with AI and machine intelligence.

5. Big Data Engineer/Architect

Big data engineers and architects play a vital role in creating the infrastructure and systems that power businesses' big data initiatives. They are tasked with designing architectures and implementing solutions that can efficiently collect, store, manage, and analyze extremely large datasets.

Some of the primary responsibilities of big data engineers and architects include:

1. Designing data architectures: They must determine how data will flow and be stored in large distributed systems. This includes choosing the appropriate storage options, file systems, databases, APIs, and frameworks to optimize for performance, scalability, and cost-efficiency.

2. Implementing data pipelines: They build data pipelines to ingest data from various sources into the big data environment. This may involve using tools like Apache Kafka, Flume, and Sqoop. They must optimize these pipelines for high throughput and fault tolerance.

3. Developing ETL processes: They design and implement extract, transform, and load (ETL) processes to move data from source systems into data warehouses and lakes. This includes writing scripts and jobs to cleanse, conform and transform data.

4. Configuring big data platforms: They deploy and configure big data platforms like Hadoop, Spark, and Hive, which allow large-scale data processing and storage. This involves setting up clusters, tuning configurations, and testing performance.

5. Integrating systems: They integrate various internal and external systems, databases, and data sources into a cohesive big-data environment so data can flow seamlessly. This requires deep knowledge of various technologies and interoperability standards.

6. Optimizing performance: They monitor the performance of the big data systems they develop, identifying bottlenecks and

optimizing for speed, reliability, and resource usage. This often involves scaling clusters up or out as needed.

Here are the steps to becoming a big data engineer or architect:

1. Get a bachelor's degree in computer science, electrical engineering, or a related quantitative field. Courses in programming, databases, data structures, and algorithms will provide a strong foundation.

2. Gain practical experience. Work on personal projects involving large datasets and open-source big data tools. Take internships or part-time roles to build your professional experience.

3. Learn key technologies. Master SQL and NoSQL databases. Learn programming languages like Python, Java, Scala, and R. Become proficient in big data frameworks like Hadoop, Spark, Hive, and Pig.

4. Learn big data architecture. Study architecture patterns used for big data systems. Understand techniques for optimizing and scaling big data pipelines. Develop an eye for performance and reliability issues.

5. Study data management. Learn ETL processes, data warehousing principles, and data modeling techniques. Understand data integration, interoperability standards, and API development.

6. Develop soft skills. Communication, collaboration, and problem-solving abilities are crucial for big data roles. Cultivate business analysis skills to understand how data solutions impact business objectives.

7. Get certified. Industry certifications like Cloudera Certified Professional Data Scientist, Hadoop Developer Certified Professional, and Certified Apache Spark Developer demonstrate your expertise and competence to employers.

Pro Tip: One way to gain experience is by volunteering to work with data for a local organization or taking on a data-focused project as part of your studies. Enrolling in a Data Science course is a plus for sure!

ChatGPT Content Creation

Step 1: Identify a Niche or Area of Interest

Decide on the type of content you want to create. This could be blog posts, eBooks, social media content, SEO articles, newsletters, or any other form of content that resonates with a specific audience. The more specific your niche, the more targeted and effective your content can be.

Step 2: Understand ChatGPT's Capabilities

Before you start creating content, take some time to understand how ChatGPT works. Experiment with different prompts to see how the AI responds and learn how to guide it to produce the content you want.

Step 3: Content Creation with ChatGPT

Start creating content using ChatGPT. Feed the AI with prompts related to your chosen niche. Review and fine-tune the generated content to make sure it aligns with your brand's voice and meets your audience's expectations.

Step 4: Monetize Your Content

There are several ways to monetize the content created by ChatGPT:

- Blogging: You can monetize your blog through affiliate marketing, sponsored posts, or ads.

- eBooks and Guides: Sell eBooks or guides on platforms like Amazon Kindle Direct Publishing, Gumroad, or your own website.

- Social Media Content: Grow your social media presence and monetize it through sponsored posts, brand collaborations, or by selling your own products or services.

- SEO Content: Drive organic traffic to your website with SEO-friendly content and increase ad revenue.

- Newsletters and Email Marketing: Use newsletters to drive traffic to monetized websites, promote affiliate products, or sell premium content.

Step 5: Scale Up

Once you start earning passive income, consider scaling up. You could create more content, explore new niches, or use ChatGPT to develop other products like chatbots or virtual assistants.

Remember, while ChatGPT can generate a wide range of content, it's important to review and fine-tune the outputs to ensure they meet your standards. With the right approach, ChatGPT can be a valuable asset in your passive income toolkit.

Case Study of an Influencer

A lifestyle influencer with a substantial following on Instagram wanted to increase engagement and monetize their account through brand collaborations and sponsored posts. However, creating unique and engaging content for daily posts and stories was time-consuming.

The influencer began using ChatGPT for generating post captions and responses to comments. They were able to feed the AI prompts related to their content - for example, "Create a motivational caption for a fitness post" or "Generate a response to a follower asking about my daily skincare routine."

Result: The influencer saw a significant boost in engagement rates, follower growth, and time saved on content creation. This increased visibility led to more brands approaching them for collaborations and sponsored posts, thus increasing their income.

Freelance Social Media Manager

A freelance social media manager handling multiple client accounts can use ChatGPT to streamline content creation. For a client in the fitness industry, ChatGPT could be prompted to generate inspiring fitness challenge posts or healthy recipe ideas. For a client in the travel industry, the AI tool could be prompted to create posts about exotic destinations or travel tips.

In all these scenarios, the key to success was not just using ChatGPT to generate content, but also reviewing and fine-tuning the output to ensure it aligns with the brand's voice and audience expectations. With the right approach, ChatGPT can be a valuable tool for creating engaging social media content and growing your digital presence.

Chapter 8: Emerging Trends in AI

This final chapter will delve into the latest trends that are shaping the landscape of Artificial Intelligence, painting a vivid picture of the transformative advancements waiting just around the corner. From breakthroughs in machine learning and natural language processing to the awe-inspiring frontiers of computer vision and robotics, you will get to witness the rapid evolution of AI and gain insight into the remarkable opportunities it presents.

Exploring Cutting-Edge AI Technologies

These are the top 10 cutting-edge AI-integrated EdTech Tools that you should try:

1. Brainly

Say hello to your new AI buddy! Brainly is the ultimate problem-solving pal. You can take advantage of its smart tech and moderating abilities to quickly give you helpful answers.

2. Cognii

Cognii makes learning easier - it's like having a great virtual tutor right by your side at all times! Cognii understands your language and provides personalized feedback and assessments for optimal growth. Plus, it can be integrated into any type of Learning Management System.

3. Duolingo

Duolingo makes learning languages fun and free. With over 40 different languages available, you'll feel like playing a game while earning points towards unlocking achievements during each course journey. Created by the brilliant minds of Luis von Ahn and Severin Hacker, Duolingo has utilized NLP chatbots that allow users to communicate within their target language along with clever ML algorithms analyzing user input which helps pinpoint mistakes as well as providing tailor-made guidance for maximum results.

4. Knewton

Knewton, established in 2008, provides students with tailored learning solutions. Leveraging AI and ML algorithms, they are able to analyze students' study habits and generate personalized content recommendations - from lesson plans to study strategies - that optimize each individual's academic journey. All of this comes together for an educational experience that feels made just for you. No more one-size fits all; Knewton has got your back when it comes to getting the most out of your studies.

5. Grammarly

Grammarly, your reliable AI-powered writing assistant! This tool is here to give you an edge in perfecting your prose and making sure every word counts. From catching pesky typos to schooling you on grammar rules, Grammarly has everything covered.

But wait, there's more; with some cutting-edge algorithms and natural language processing, this powerhouse will analyze all of your text in real-time, giving precious feedback on how to improve any document or email masterpiece – no matter the genre you write in. Students, professionals, and writers alike are making this their go-to when they need wordsmithing help.

6. Quillbot

Quillbot is a revolutionary AI-powered paraphrasing tool. Whether you need help with one sentence or an entire article, this innovative technology has got your back. It quickly understands your content and provides relevant rephrasings that will take your writing to new heights. And don't forget about its modes like conventional, fluency, formal, simple, and imaginative - just choose what works best for you.

Quillbot doesn't stop there. It also broadens your vocabulary and generates logical pieces of text. Plus? You can adjust the synonym usage as much as you'd like until you get exactly what you need.

7. Speechify

Say goodbye to boring lectures and tedious studying - Speechify is here to revolutionize your learning experience. This AI tool has the power to transform any written text into audio, allowing you to absorb educational material with ease.

From short notes and long paragraphs, all the way up to entire books - Speechify can handle it all without breaking a sweat. So forget about straining your eyes from reading for hours on end; now is the time to kick back, relax, and let this amazing technology do its thing!

8. Nearpod

Ready to take your learning experience to the next level? Look no further than Nearpod – an AI-powered platform that will blow you away with its virtual reality, 3D models, and incredible group activities. This tool is designed to give you a dynamic and engaging education that's sure to leave lasting impressions.

9. StepWise Math

If math has been giving you trouble, say hello to StepWise Math – it'll make all those tricky equations seem simple in no time, thanks to its personalized instructions and feedback powered by state-of-the-art AI technology. Get ready for an out-of-this-world tutoring journey as you work towards solving all your math problems with ease.

AI and the Internet of Things (IoT)

The Internet of Things (IoT) facilitates the connection of billions of devices, industrial machinery, processes, and users to share data seamlessly without centralized control. However, managing large data sets is extremely intricate during storage, processing, and inference.

Therefore, AI has emerged as a highly promising combination with IoT to improve data usage, storage, and decision-making by mitigating uncertainty. AI plays a significant role in IoT. It enhances the value of diverse data types collected by IoT devices.

Proper utilization of this diverse data offers efficient solutions for product plus service development that meet user expectations across various sectors. Despite the various benefits of integrating AI with intelligent systems for industrial applications, applying AI effectively presents challenges related to data quality, volume, integration, and accuracy of inferences.

ML methods and technologies have emerged in AI in recent years: the convergence of ML and IoT will mutually enhance the impact and availability of services in areas like healthcare, supply chain, transportation, and power sectors.

Quantum Computing: Unleashing the Power within AI

Quantum computing is not your everyday run-of-the-mill computing. It goes beyond the ordinary and delves into the wondrous world of atoms and molecules. But hold on to your hats because it doesn't stop there! It takes a closer look at the teeny-tiny subatomic properties of atoms that can actually be in multiple states at the same time. These quantum mechanics principles let subatomic particles exist as both particles and waves simultaneously.

Now, these principles might seem a bit out of place in computing. Then, why is this even a thing? Well, they throw the traditional "binary bits" (that is the 0's and 1's) out the window. Quantum computers can store and process data not only in the "on" or "off" states but also in superposed combinations. By harnessing these principles, quantum computers can quickly crack complex problems.

How does that benefit you? It means they can uncover hidden patterns in behemoth-sized data sets that stumped conventional computers! Prepare to have your mind blown - because quantum computers are truly in a league of their own.

And guess what? AI just got a serious upgrade. Quantum computing can analyze a wide range of data types and reach more accurate conclusions than present-day computers. While those regular computers are stuck in the binary universe, quantum computers can process information with "qubits" that can exist in multiple states all at once. The result? A quantum leap in data analysis and smarter, more insightful conclusions.

So buckle up because quantum computing is here to revolutionize the way the mysteries of the universe are tackled; it's time to unleash its power and embark on an extraordinary journey through the quantum realm. Get ready for a computing experience like no other!

How Will Quantum Computing Change AI?

AI has really come a long way. It can whip up realistic 3D images and videos, and now it's getting cozy with quantum computing. Yes, that's right-quantum AI is on the horizon. AI has now tapped into the power of quantum computers, and let me tell you, this integration is going to be mind-blowing!

This next section will be all about the advantages of using quantum AI in creative industries.

Edge Computing in AI

Feeling overwhelmed? Let Edge AI be your digital sidekick! Combining Edge Computing and Artificial Intelligence, this tech supercharges your device with lightning-fast data processing. No internet connection is necessary - you can get instant results without waiting for a slow response from the cloud. Plus, its ML algorithms are incredibly energy efficient.

Unraveling the Magic of Edge AI

So what's so great about Edge AI? It creates an intelligent system right on your own hardware that can analyze data in real time. With it powering up your gadgets and machines, you'll experience ultra-smart performance like never before. Think of it as having a tiny computer inside each one of them, making decisions quickly and accurately!

There's something truly magical about harnessing the power of edge computing with Artificial Intelligence – especially when put into action by savvy machine learning algorithms. Its ability to deliver immediate analytics is seriously impressive while reducing lag significantly – talk about speed demon efficiency levels!

And don't forget: these powerful programs work on all sorts of devices, big or small - just like Iron Man's Jarvis but way cooler (and less expensive!). So, if you want superhuman smartness ready at your fingertips 24/7, then look no further than

Edge AI; let its awesomeness take over, and watch how things start going more smoothly immediately.

Unveiling the Secrets of Edge AI Software

Ready to explore the incredible world of Edge AI software? Think of it as a hidden chest packed with unbelievable ML algorithms that can do some mind-blowing stuff on your device - no internet connection/remote servers required! You will be astonished by real-time data like never before; just forget about having to use extra systems.

Exploring the Wonders of Edge AI Hardware

Edge AI can conquer any hardware platform, from regular MCUs to super-advanced neural processing devices. These devices use embedded algorithms to monitor their behavior, collect and process data and make decisions. And the best part? They do it all without needing a human touch.

Smartphones, laptops, smart cars, and Raspberry PIs are just a few examples of the star-studded lineup of Edge AI devices.

Discovering the Benefits of Edge AI

With Edge AI, data is processed locally, eliminating the time-consuming back-and-forth with the cloud. Real-time analytics become a breeze as high-performance computing meets sensors and IoT devices on the edge.

Say goodbye to sluggish processing speeds. Edge AI turbocharges your data processing; the data is processed right where it's generated, resulting in lightning-fast speeds. Speaking of speeds, Edge AI significantly reduces bandwidth requirements and costs - by processing data locally, it cuts down on the need for hefty internet bandwidth and expensive cloud storage.

Data security gets an upgrade with Edge AI. With most data processing happening on the edge device itself, sensitive information stays far away from the prying eyes of cyber-criminals.

When it comes to scalability, Edge AI is a heavyweight. It effortlessly handles vast amounts of data - so there's no need to simultaneously burden the cloud with transferring video image data from multiple sources.

Reliability gets a boost with Edge AI. The combination of heightened security and lightning-fast speed ensures a seamless and trustworthy experience with your Edge AI system.

Say hello to cost efficiency! AI processing at the edge is incredibly cost-effective, as only the essential and valuable data is sent to the cloud - no more wasting resources on unnecessary data.

Edge AI Examples

Edge artificial intelligence (AI) refers to the use of AI and machine learning models at the edge of the network, closest to where data is generated and actions must be taken. Rather than sending all data to the cloud for processing, edge AI performs computational tasks locally - on IoT devices, mobile devices, gateways, or micro data centers.

Edge AI offers various benefits, like lower latency, reduced bandwidth usage, improved privacy and security, and the ability to operate independently without an internet connection. As a result, it is being adopted across multiple industries and use cases.

Industrial IoT remains a major focus for edge AI, with edge devices acting as 'brains' for sensors that monitor equipment health, detect anomalies and enable predictive maintenance. However, edge AI solutions are also being applied in DevOps, using AI models to identify anomalies and optimize code deployment processes.

Edge AI is also powering the next generation of consumer devices, from smartphones with faster face recognition to smart home assistants with always-on capabilities. Edge AI is even enabling new frontiers in robotics research by allowing robots to process sensor data, make inferences and take actions in real time.

Amazing Health Monitoring Devices

Want to bring the power of AI to the world of healthcare but don't want to compromise patient privacy? Well, guess what? Edge AI is here to save the day! With this awesome technology, hospitals and healthcare providers can analyze all that valuable data from health monitoring devices right on the premises - this means real-time analytics for better patient care while keeping their privacy intact!

Edge AI Software Like No Other

Allsbrook is a company that specializes in implementing edge AI in industrial IoT devices. Their platform, Onyx, allows companies to make sense of all that live IoT data without having to go through the hassle of creating new models or hiring countless data scientists. Plus, it's so flexible that it supports multiple languages and various tools.

Self-Driving Cars

Say goodbye to the days of manual driving - self-driving cars are here and they're making waves on the roads with their cutting-edge AI capabilities. They can stay one step ahead of any tricky situation, ensuring your ride is safe and reliable every time you get behind the wheel.

Security Cameras

Thanks to their sophisticated Edge AI technology, you won't believe what these security cameras can do: detect objects, recognize faces, and even have two-way audio for when you need to hear what's happening outside your home or business. Vmukti has some seriously impressive models that make surveillance easy.

Smart Homes are Here to Stay

The ultimate smart home setup isn't just a dream anymore - it's totally achievable with Edge AI taking over all data processing needs right there at your doorstep with voice-controlled lightbulbs, video doorbells that sync up with fridges, and more working together seamlessly.

Generative AI: Creating Music, Art, and Literature

Generative AI is the game-changer everyone has been waiting for; it's revolutionizing how art, music, and literature are created and enjoyed. With mind-blowing technology at its core, generative AI uses algorithms to conjure up new and exciting content - unleashing a world of possibilities for artists, musicians, and writers.

Thanks to generative AI, artists can create mind-blowing masterpieces that blend traditional techniques seamlessly with cutting-edge technology. By training neural networks on thousands of images, anyone can now whip up incredible works that fuse different styles and genres. The result? A kaleidoscope of AI-generated art (including abstract wonders and incredibly lifelike portraits).

Literature is no exception to the generative AI magic - by training neural networks with heaps of text, these models can spin enchanting stories, heartwarming poems, and thought-provoking essays. It's incredible how they manage to keep everything so coherent and engaging. AI-generated novels are now making their mark on the literary scene.

AI is even diving into journalism - rapidly generating news articles and reports in the blink of an eye. Not to mention, generative AI is also breathing life into video games and virtual reality experiences - crafting immersive narratives that adapt to the user's choices. It's storytelling on steroids.

Now, onto the music industry: Brace yourself because generative AI is turning composers and musicians into wizards. With their ability to analyze musical patterns, these AI systems are composing completely original tunes - and even full albums. The melodies, harmonies, and rhythms they create are both exceptional and delightful to hear. So picture musicians are teaming up with AI to create mind-bending compositions that defy the norms of traditional music-making! Plus, generative AI is also curating personalized playlists and even dreaming up new instruments - music lovers, get ready for an audio revolution.

But that's not all. Generative AI is even flexing its creative muscles in fashion, architecture, and product design. So, brace yourself for a creative revolution like no other; generative AI is here to blow your mind, shift boundaries, and make the impossible possible. The future of art, music, and literature has never looked more exciting.

AI and Human-Machine Integration

Ever heard of HMI? It's all about humans and machines having a blast together through a user interface. Think expressions, gestures, and even funky dance moves! These natural and intuitive interactions are gaining popularity, making it easier to control computer systems.

HMI is making moves in the healthcare world. With HMI, doctors and specialists can give spot-on assessments and personalized treatment plans for their patients, making healthcare way cooler!

But wait, there's more! HMI is here to save the day in manufacturing too. HMI can eliminate complexity and errors by combining human expertise with machine precision, boosting efficiency to the max.

Can you picture the future of HMI? As technology keeps evolving, HMI is going to change everything.

The following are some of the things HMI is set to change:

Augmented Reality:

Time to blend reality and virtual magic! Augmented reality (AR) mixes real-world stuff with computer-generated goodness to create an interactive experience like no other. AR is changing the game in healthcare, manufacturing, and even education by projecting digital info onto the real world.

Natural Language Processing:

Natural Language Processing (NLP) is all about teaching computers to understand and chat as humans do. I

Robotics:

The world of robotics is basically a playground for creating the most efficient machines. From assembly lines to hospitals and even roads, these bots are here to lend a helping hand. They keep leveling up their intelligence and becoming more flexible.

Collaborative Intelligence:

Are humans and AI teaming up? That's the magic of Collaborative Intelligence - it's all about combining human ability with AI to conquer colossal challenges and achieve shared dreams. Whether it's cracking complex puzzles or simply crafting mesmerizing art, this partnership is launching humanity to new dimensions of greatness.

Smart Homes:

Welcome to the future, where homes are smarter than ever! Connected to the internet, homes became a breeze to control. From flicking lights to adjusting the perfect temperature, you can do it all from afar.

AI in Space Exploration and Colonization

Forget human astronauts - AI has arrived to take humanity on a journey to explore the beyond. With its mind-boggling autonomous machines, humanity can now make incredible strides in understanding the mysteries of space.

These advanced robots are more than capable of venturing into unknown territories and uncovering fascinating information about distant planets and stars. They provide data that is truly out of this world! And if that wasn't enough, these droids also help create ultra-smart spacecraft which have been designed to fly through space without needing any human navigation whatsoever.

AI isn't just making cosmic discoveries easier; it's revolutionizing how spaceships are operated. This technology helps scientists automate operations, crunch massive amounts of data quickly, and even save lives when needed. So don't be surprised when you see stories hitting the headlines all around the universe —the age-old dream of exploring space has finally become an amazing reality thanks to Artificial Intelligence.

Rovers

AI-equipped Rovers (like the Mars Exploration Rover and Curiosity) have been fearlessly venturing through the rough terrains of Mars for many years.

These smart rovers detect potential dangers lurking in their uninhabited surroundings; they can spot treacherous rocks and daunting craters. And here is the real shocker; they use AI to process all the collected data and calculate the best/safest path.

AEGIS is also making its grand entry into the cosmic arena. It's a groundbreaking innovation that takes us to a breathtaking world where rovers scour the planetary surface in search of extraordinary rocks to investigate and explore.

Satellite Operations

AI is taking satellite operations to a whole new level by producing efficient, smart, and fast solutions for managing satellites.

Starting with SpaceX, their navigation satellites are like "space acrobats." They analyze data from the satellite's sensors, like its position and velocity to figure out if there's any potential danger coming their way. And guess what? They don't just sit there and wait for disaster to strike; they actually take some evasive action - the satellite's onboard computer jumps in, takes control, and adjusts the speed/direction of the satellite in order to avoid collision.

AI can even make the process of maneuvering satellites into their correct orbits a piece of cake! But how? By optimizing it, of course. Using AI can reduce the amount of fuel needed and the time it takes to get those satellites exactly where they need to be in space.

Data Analysis

By using AI, you can say goodbye to outdated and time-consuming data analysis techniques. With the help of powerful ML algorithms, you can analyze data from space missions faster and with incredible precision. Satellites, probes, and other cosmic tools will spill their secrets as we identify hidden patterns - plus unveil potential discoveries or dangers lurking within the data.

There is even more: AI has the power to unravel data trends and provide even deeper insights through its predictive analytics and forecasting capabilities.

Planetary Geology (Astrogeology)

Thanks to AI, scientists have unlocked an incredible superpower: spotting and labeling all the geological features on other planets and moons. Craters, volcanoes - you name it! But that's not even the best part. This tech can create 3D models of extraterrestrial terrain with amazing detail. So why is this so important? Well, these ultra-detailed maps help scientists get a better understanding of how those environments evolved over time – which could completely change current knowledge about space exploration.

Rocket Landing

SpaceX is going above and beyond to make rocket landings cooler than ever. Thanks to cutting-edge AI, they are able to crunch all the complex data from the sensors and telemetry systems. This helps them control the rocket's trajectory with laser precision and even automate certain parts of the landing process, like controlling those powerful engines or deploying landing gear at just the right moment.

Star and Galaxy Mapping

To top off this already amazing feat, astronomers can now use these same algorithms for galactic mapping purposes. It's almost as if they have a cheat sheet from outer space that allows them to accurately identify stars and galaxies and predict their behavior in advance.

Predictive Maintenance

You know how AI is great at crunching data? It's also very good at spotting potential problems and recommending preventative maintenance.

ChatGPT, trained on a diverse range of internet text, can be utilized to analyze technical manuals, maintenance records, and various sensor data. Using this information, it can identify patterns and correlations that may indicate an impending failure or the need for maintenance - even before any signs of problems become apparent to human operators.

This predictive capability can result in substantial cost savings, as it allows for timely maintenance that can prevent expensive repairs or replacements down the line. But it's not just about saving money - predictive maintenance can also contribute significantly to safety. By identifying and addressing potential issues before they escalate, the risk of accidents or failures that could endanger human lives can be mitigated.

AI in Transhumanism

The captivating narratives of HAL 9000, the Terminator, and Frankenstein have all held us in thrall, serving as cautionary tales about the perils of rapid technological advancement. But what does the future hold? As we approach 2045, Ray Kurzweil makes a daring prediction: computers will surpass human intelligence. While we muse on these AI representations in fiction, let's delve into an even darker territory: transhumanism.

Rather than fretting over machines becoming excessively human, consider the inverse: humans becoming excessively machine-like. It's crucial to find the right equilibrium between humanity and technology, so brace yourselves - we need to stay ahead of the curve!

Transhumanists theorize the feasibility of transferring human consciousness into machines, promising a form of eternal life. Tech titan Elon Musk is even working on brain-computer interfaces to facilitate human-robot interaction. However, this trajectory could lead to a future where humans become redundant.

We're at a juncture, with AI and transhumanism on one side and an uncertain future on the other. Giant corporations wield algorithms that predict our every move, but there's no need for despair - regaining your autonomy is still within reach.

To reclaim control, we must explore and understand new technologies while safeguarding our intrinsic human qualities, such as independent thought. Each day brings us deeper insights into technology's capabilities - but the choice of how it will be used rests with you. Will it be a force for good, or will it lead to our downfall? ChatGPT, with its human-like conversational abilities, is a prime example of such technology that can be used to benefit humanity, rather than threaten it.

Future of ChatGPT

More human-like conversation - ChatGPT will continue to become better at understanding context, nuance, and producing more human-sounding responses. The goal is to make communicating with AI indistinguishable from humans.

- Integration into more applications: ChatGPT's capabilities will be integrated into many different apps and interfaces. For example, AI writing assistants, code autocompletion tools, educational apps, etc.

- Generative creativity: ChatGPT shows potential for AI to be creative and generative beyond just mimicking human language. It may be able to generate music, images, and even new ideas in the future.

- Democratization of knowledge: ChatGPT makes vast amounts of information accessible to anyone for free. This could greatly expand opportunities for learning and problem-solving.

- Impact on work: AI assistants like ChatGPT could take over many repetitive information-based jobs like customer service, report writing, etc. It may displace many white-collar workers.

- Goal-aligned intelligence: Future AI systems need alignment to human values and goals. ChatGPT shows risks of AI not having a unified objective. Safeguards will need to be developed.

- Regulation debates: As capabilities increase, there will be debates around regulation, like monitoring for misuse, limiting areas AI can operate, etc. Difficult tradeoffs will need to be made.

- Determining truth: ChatGPT sometimes generates plausible-sounding but false information. Future systems will need robust methods for distinguishing truth and falsehoods.

Conclusion

"Unlocking Passive Income with ChatGPT" explores the transformative power of AI and its immense potential to shape the future. Throughout this book, you have witnessed the remarkable advancements in AI technology and its widespread impact on various industries and aspects of human life.

This book has highlighted how AI is revolutionizing industries such as healthcare, finance, transportation, and manufacturing, unlocking new opportunities for efficiency, productivity, and profitability. By automating repetitive tasks, analyzing vast amounts of data, and making accurate predictions, AI has proven itself to be a valuable tool for businesses to gain a competitive edge and drive innovation.

Moreover, the book emphasizes the symbiotic relationship between AI and human intelligence. Instead of replacing humans, AI acts as a powerful assistant, augmenting capabilities and enabling people to focus on complex problem-solving, creativity, and strategic thinking. It has the potential to free humanity from mundane tasks, allowing it to explore new frontiers of knowledge and contribute to the betterment of society.

However, it also acknowledges the ethical and societal challenges that arise with the rapid advancement of AI. It calls for responsible development, ensuring transparency, fairness, and accountability in AI systems to avoid potential biases and unintended consequences. It urges policymakers, researchers, and industry leaders to collaborate in establishing robust frameworks and guidelines to govern AI's deployment and mitigate any potential risks.

Ultimately, "Unlocking Passive Income with ChatGPT" paints a hopeful picture of the future, where AI-driven technologies continue to accelerate human progress, fuel economic growth, and enhance our overall well-being. It stresses the importance of embracing AI as a catalyst for positive change while upholding ethical values and ensuring that the benefits are accessible to all.

Thank You

I greatly appreciate your decision to purchase my book, "Unlocking Passive Income with ChatGPT". Amidst numerous options, you took a leap of faith and chose this book, for which I am deeply grateful.

Thank you for your engagement and for making it through to the very end.

Before you sign off, I humbly request a little favor from you. **Could you consider leaving a review on the respective platform? Offering your thoughts in a review is the most effective way to support the endeavors of independent authors like myself.**

Your valuable input will motivate me to continue producing content that aids in achieving your desired outcomes. Your feedback will be deeply cherished.

\>> Kindly leave a review on Amazon <<

References

Asare, J.G. The Dark Side Of ChatGPT; Forbes: Jersey City, NJ, USA, 2023. Available online: https://www.forbes.com/sites/janicegassam/2023/01/28/the-dark-side-of-chatgpt/?sh=31f2e08a4799

Check Point Research. OPWNAI: Cybercriminals Starting to Use chatGPT. Checkpoint.com. 2023. Available online: https://research. checkpoint.com/2023/opwnai-cybercriminals-starting-to-use-chatgpt/

Getahun, H. ChatGPT Could Be Used for Good, But Like Many Other AI Models, It's Rife with Racist and Discriminatory Bias; Insider. 2023. Available online: https://www.insider.com/chatgpt-is-like-many-other-ai-models-rife-with-bias-2023-1

Heaven, W.D. How ChatGPT works and AI, ML and NLP Fundamentals. Mit Technol. Rev. 2023. Available online: https://www.technologyreview.com/2023/02/08/1068068/chatgpt-is-everywhere-heres-where-it-came-from/

Hutanu, A. How ChatGPT Works and AI, ML and NLP Fundamentals. PentaBlog. 2023. Available online: https://www.pentalog. com/blog/tech-trends/chatgpt-fundamentals/#:~:text=ChatGPT%20is%20an%20AI%20language,text%20data%20to%20 generate%20language

King, M.R.; ChatGPT. A Conversation on Artificial Intelligence, Chatbots, and Plagiarism in Higher Education. Cell. Mol. Bioeng. 2023, 16, 1–2. [CrossRef] [PubMed]

Lund, B.D.; Wang, T. Chatting about ChatGPT: How may AI and GPT impact academia and libraries? Library Hi Tech News 2023, in press. [CrossRef]

Marr, B. Will ChatGPT Put Data Analysts Out Of Work? Forbes: Jersey City, NJ, USA, 2023. Available online: https://www.forbes.com/sites/bernardmarr/2023/02/07/will-chatgpt-put-data-analysts-out-of-work/?sh=46433cf64030

Mollick, E. ChatGPT Is a Tipping Point for AI; Harvard Business Review: Brighton, MA, USA, 2022. Available online: https://hbr.org/20 22/12/chatgpt-is-a-tipping-point-for-ai

Przybyla, M. Why ChatGPT Is Good for the Data Science Community. Medium. 2023. Available online: https://medium.com/ geekculture/why-chatgpt-is-good-for-the-data-science-community-d4dfbebb4ef

van Dis, A.M.; Bollen, J.; Zuidema, W.; van Rooji, R.; Bockting, C.L. ChatGPT: Five priorities for research. Nature 2023. Available online: https://www.nature.com/articles/d41586-023-00288-7

Made in United States
Troutdale, OR
11/19/2023

14754013R00124